The Rye Bread Marriage

The Rye Bread Marriage

HOW I FOUND HAPPINESS WITH A PARTNER I'LL NEVER UNDERSTAND

MICHAELE WEISSMAN

ALGONQUIN BOOKS
OF CHAPEL HILL
2023

Published by
ALGONQUIN BOOKS OF CHAPEL HILL
Post Office Box 2225
Chapel Hill, North Carolina 27515-2225

an imprint of WORKMAN PUBLISHING CO., INC.,
a subsidiary of HACHETTE BOOK GROUP, INC.
1290 Avenue of the Americas
New York, NY 10104

Printed in the United States of America.
Design by Steve Godwin.

The publisher is not responsible for websites
(or their content) that are not owned by the publisher.

Library of Congress Cataloging-in-Publication Data

Names: Weissman, Michaele, author.
Title: The rye bread marriage / Michaele Weissman.
Description: First edition. | Chapel Hill : Algonquin Books of
Chapel Hill, 2023. | Includes bibliographical references. |
Summary: "When the author's Latvia-born husband, John,
opens a company marketing rye bread, the author embarks on
a European journey in search of John's origins, excavating poignant
stories of war, privation, and resilience"— Provided by publisher.
Identifiers: LCCN 2023008108 | ISBN 9781643752693 (hardcover) |
ISBN 9781643755243 (ebook)
Subjects: LCSH: Melngailis, John, [date]– | Melngailis family. |
Latvian Americans—United States—Biography. | Weissman,
Michaele—Marriage. | Jews—United States—Biography. | Immigrants—
Massachusetts—Biography. | Rye bread—United States. | Physicists—
United States—Biography. | Journalists—United States—Biography.
Classification: LCC E184.L4 M459 2023 |
DDC 305.89193/073—dc23/eng/20230301
LC record available at https://lccn.loc.gov/2023008108

10 9 8 7 6 5 4 3 2 1
First Edition

To our children and our children's children

This is a work of nonfiction. Some names have
been changed to protect privacy or save feelings.
The timeline is true. There are no composite characters.
In some cases, dialogue has been reconstructed.

CONTENTS

PART ONE

You Wake Up Married   1

PART TWO

A Displaced Person   79

PART THREE

A Rye Bread Marriage   143

Epilogue   265
Acknowledgments   267
Notes   271

PART ONE

You Wake Up Married

1. What You Love Tells Everything About You

Latvia is a place where people love rye bread. They sing songs about rye bread. Babies teethe on it. Legend has it that the country's first president never ate a meal without a slice of Latvia's signature sourdough rye, called *rupjmaize*. Supermarkets allot row after row of shelf space to rye bread. Rye bread competitions for amateur and professional bakers are a big deal in Latvia: winners give teary speeches hailing their bread baking teachers. In Latvia you can buy ice cream flavored with rye breadcrumbs. Yogurt, too. One of the country's most popular tourist destinations is a kind of rye-bread Disney World with a bakery to tour, playgrounds, picnic areas, restaurants, stores, and a special room where newlyweds can bake their first loaf of rye bread together. If you were born in Latvia or if you are of Latvian parentage, you have no manifest destiny to embrace. History has not been kind to your people. What you have, instead, is a mystical connection to the grain-bearing earth. What you have is rye bread.

2. You Wake Up Married to a Stranger

You wake up one morning married to a stranger who loves

Latvian rye bread. This dense, dark sourdough whispers of damp forest floors and peasant farmers swinging scythes through ancient fields of rye. Black-crusted and hearty, Latvian rye bread feeds your husband's body and his soul. It is a touchstone of his fractured identity. A talisman of his always-present past.

You thought you were marrying a European who loved food, a *feinschmecker* fluent in languages who would turn you into a world traveler. You do travel together, that is true, but before marrying you did not understand the depth of your future husband's foreignness—nor could you know then that his sense of displacement would increase over time. He is not a Western European or a Northern European. He is an Eastern European refugee, one of the perpetually dispossessed, whose pasts follow behind like the tails of kites flapping noisily in the wind.

Moreover, he is a man of staunch opinions. Do you as his wife share his passion for Latvian rye bread? For many years his vehemence leaves little room for you to discover how you feel about Latvian rye bread, or Latvia for that matter.

Before you marry, you assume his foreignness will wane. You think he will become like you, no longer yearning for rye bread or his homeland.

In retrospect you marvel at your own naiveté.

Again and again you ask yourself how this happened. The answer never changes. You felt compelled to be near him. You wanted to die in his arms. He reminded you of a film noir hero in a belted trench standing under a streetlight. You loved his long, triangulated chest. His haunches. The smell of him.

Even when you wish he were different, you admire him.

His high standards. His fundamental decency. So many years together and your respect does not waver.

Nor does the boomeranging quality of your mutual attraction.

You were flattered that he came and found you fourteen years after you met. You find it comforting that he remembered you and pursued you. You never question that he loves you. But none of that can bridge the gap between you. He is so Latvian, so wrapped up in the history and culture of a tiny captive land that few can locate on a map. And you, you are so expansively American—American and Jewish. Your grandparents did not yearn for the old country. They preferred an America of fatty brisket, roast chicken, Chinese food, and fluffy challah without a gram of roughage. Also, ice cream. When he complains that the hand-dipped strawberry in his dish is too rich (he always orders strawberry in a dish, not a cone, which just goes to show) you ask him how ice cream can possibly be too rich. You might as well ask how sourdough rye, so puckery and tough, can be an object of his desire.

You wake up married to a rye-bread-loving stranger, and slowly you realize that your husband doesn't want to be like you and he isn't going to become like you. In fact, he wants you to be like him! From this nexus of unresolvable difference the decades-long battle is engaged. You fight about the thermostat and the thickness of the towels. You fight about the morality of French toast and buying new shoes for the baby. You fight about money. You fight about World War II and who sold out whom. Usually the fights are more stupid than cruel, but not always. Sometimes he is mean. Sometimes you are mean. Still you wake up snuggling skin to skin—he burns hot and never wears pajamas. Even in the winter.

In time you realize this whirling dervish of mixed emotion, of love and fury, of compatibility, attraction, tenderness, and contention: this is your life and your marriage. Your Rye Bread Marriage. You wonder what it would be like to be married to someone who is your twin. Who does not look down on your love of comfort (while nonetheless benefiting from it). Who is able to leave home without a five-pound loaf of Latvian rye bread crowding the shirts and shoes in his carry-on. Someone for whom rye bread is not the answer to every question. But that is not the case. You are married to him and he is married to you, and for better and for worse he loves you and you love him. And it is your peculiar fate to spend a lifetime trying to figure out what that means. And so, this book. This exploration of bread and marriage, of history, identity, and all that the heart holds dear. After a lifetime of telling other people's stories, you have come full circle and now, to your surprise, you are telling his story, and your story, too.

3. Marriage: First Definition

Marriage: A common skin enveloping two separate beings who shape each other's lives and impact each other's concerns and interests. This semi-permeable membrane nourished by memories of a shared romantic past evolves continually and yet, paradoxically, remains constant.

4. Summer Romance (Cambridge, Massachusetts, July 1967)

We met at a party in Harvard Square. He was a physicist with a PhD, newly hired at MIT's Lincoln Lab. I was a rising senior at Brandeis living at home between semesters, working a nothing summer job. He was twenty-eight. I was twenty.

He said his name was John Melngailis.

"Meln Guy Lis," I repeated, melding the *l* and *n* as he did.

"You've got a good ear," he said.

"And that's not all," I said.

He asked about my name. Michaele, pronounced Michael.

"My parents wanted a son," I told him, adding that I had six older sisters and that my parents had gotten tired of waiting.

"Really?"

"Not really. I'm the middle of three girls. But it's true they wanted a boy."

John raised his bushy eyebrows, but said nothing. He was tall and slender, with blond hair and a shaggy mustache. His face was angular. Nordic. With slate-blue eyes. He spoke English with a barely discernible accent. I thought he was gorgeous.

"What do physicists do?" I asked.

"We measure natural phenomena. Surface acoustic waves. That sort of thing."

I told him I was studying medieval history.

"Why would you do that," he asked.

"I want to write a book about Abelard and Héloïse," I said.

"Who?"

I told him about the birth of romantic love in twelfth-century France. I told him that I believed Héloïse and Abelard were intellectual partners as well as lovers. "Her family's henchmen castrated him. She fled to a monastery and stayed there for the rest of her life," I added.

"I hate the Catholic church," he said.

"Don't you believe in Western Civilization?" I asked, suddenly earnest.

"No, not really," he said. "I'm a pagan."

John took my cigarette out of my hand. He inhaled in an exaggerated way and blew smoke rings in my face, reminding me of Jean-Paul Belmondo in *Breathless*.

I drank vodka tonics. He drank gin rickeys. He spoke to me in French—he had just returned from a year as a postdoc in Paris. I understood half of what he said.

When we slow-danced, I pressed my hips against his, threw my head back, and laughed. A move I'd learned from the movies. I guess it worked because he called the next day. Would I like to go swimming on Sunday?

At eleven on Sunday the doorbell rang. I stuffed my swimsuit, towel, and makeup bag into my large purple tote and raced down the stairs.

As we *vroom-vroom*ed north in his yellow VW Beetle, John told me about living in Europe. He was even more urbane than my comp lit teacher, who served quiche at his parties.

John spied the sign he was looking for. We took a sharp right off the highway and soon we were bumping along a dirt road, passing campsites, food shacks, and towels hanging on clotheslines. Eventually, we arrived at an unpopulated spot and John pulled the car into a clearing where it couldn't be seen from the road.

Swim before lunch? he asked.

We changed into our suits out of sight of each other. I was wearing a tame one-piece. John wore a navy-blue speedo. He looked me up and down. Then he lifted me up and carried me into the water. Real life for one moment surpassed my Technicolor fantasies. We swam to an island in the middle of the lake, where we made out on a sun-warmed slab of granite. When we returned to shore, John gathered kindling. He cut branches with the axe he kept in his trunk. Then he built a fire and grilled lamb chops. He opened a bottle of Château-Lafite Rothschild 1963. Not a great year, but definitely a great move.

What followed was a perfect summer romance. In addition to his good looks, John was interesting. He had a story. He'd been born in Latvia on the eve of World War II. His childhood memories seemed to exist as a series of still photographs from a World War II documentary: the pretty white house in the countryside where he lived with his parents and brother. The garden filled with fruit trees and bushes laden with red and black currants. The young German soldiers who commandeered his house, operating a communications center in the basement. The Russian bombs that exploded in the garden. The ships filled with Latvian families fleeing westward *toward* Germany, to escape the Russians.

That's the part I got hung up on: That his parents fled *to* Germany. They weren't Jewish, of course, but still. How could it be that Hitler's Germany, the very heart of darkness, was for John's family a place of refuge? I understood in theory that Latvians and other Eastern Europeans considered Stalin, not Hitler, to be history's greatest villain. I understood, but not really.

John took me to a Latvian folk music concert where he seemed to know everyone in the audience. He described Latvia as a "captive nation." He talked about being a Latvian activist. He talked about the dreams of the Latvian community in America for the restoration of the Latvian republic. He talked about the Latvian rye bread baked by his mother. He wanted me to taste it. When John said "we" he meant "we Latvians," not "we Americans."

All summer I reveled in John's attention, without understanding it. In my mind, our romance was a prelude to the glamorous life I would lead after I graduated from college and moved to New York. That John took our relationship seriously—that he was in love with me—did not register. The sexual revolution: that was my generation's gift to the world. The idea of marriage struck me as preposterous.

By November, I had grown weary of John's devotion. I am too young, and you are too Latvian, I said when I dumped him. (No one quite so unkind as an inexperienced lover.)

5. New York Bathtub (West Eighty-fourth Street, 1981)

I graduated from Brandeis and moved to NYC. I worked for a radio station and discovered the women's movement. My best friend, Carol Hymowitz, and I wrote a book called *A History of Women in America*. We both had jobs. We wrote on our time off. The book took seven years to write. After it was published, I wrote many magazine and newspaper articles. John married Liz, the roommate of the woman who hosted the party where we met. They had two daughters and stayed married for thirteen years. I didn't give much thought to marrying until my early thirties when I found myself standing in the checkout line at Safeway making goo-goo eyes at babies. When baby hunger finally hit me, it hit hard.

One night, submerged in my bathtub on West Eighty-fourth Street staring at the black-and-white subway tiles on the wall, my mind wandered to all the men I had slept with. Which of them, I wondered, might be good father material? That's when I thought of John. How kind he was. How safe he made me feel.

A few weeks later, John called. Just like that. He told me he had been keeping track of my whereabouts in the Manhattan phone directory. He and Liz were getting divorced, he reported. He was coming to New York to attend a conference at the end of the month and wondered if I would have dinner with him.

I had seen John and Liz a few times after I moved to New York. Visiting friends in Cambridge, I had attended more than one dinner party at their house. Once they fixed me up with a French scientist who happened to be in town. This was in 1973, the same year Russell Baker wrote a column in the *New York Times* making fun of the cluelessness of young people like me who considered "jealousy [to be] hopelessly passé and . . . tiresome." I appreciated Liz and John's hospitality and I liked Liz, but to me they seemed oddly out of sync as a couple, as if they were in two different movies. It did not occur to me that I considered Liz a rival. Eventually the three of us lost touch.

"I'm not surprised you're getting divorced," I blurted out. Then I told him I would love to have dinner with him.

6. First Date, Second Time (New York, 1982)

He showed up at my door with a bunch of yellow freesia.

He was handsome as ever.

He had made a reservation at a northern Italian boîte tucked under the Queensboro Bridge on the East Side of Manhattan. The kind of place where the waiters came from Calabria, not acting school.

"Which do you think is sexier, French food or Italian food?" I asked, as we sipped sambuca after dinner.

"Depends on who you are with," John answered.

On our cab ride back to the West Side, John spoke Russian with the cabdriver. As in the past, I was a sucker for his brand of showing off. When we climbed out of the cab in front of my building, there was no doubt he would spend the night.

The following afternoon, bleary-eyed and happy, we traipsed upstairs to the sixth floor to drink sherry with Harry and BD—the big-hearted leftie intellectuals I had adopted as wannabe parents, preferring their lifestyle to that of my suburban mother and father. (I didn't hate my parents. I hated golf.)

Leaning back against the couch, listening to BD talk about the play she and Harry had seen the night before, overhearing John and Harry talking about physics, I let myself go, falling into a fog of what? Love? Infatuation? Sleeplessness? Baby craving? I heard John comment on the chessboard in the corner. John and Harry agreed to play when John next returned to New York.

Harry and BD hugged me warmly on our way out the door. I could see in their eyes I had done good. A physicist. And a chess-playing physicist at that. (I would have won the trifecta if he played the violin.)

7. Comice Pears

One Sunday morning when John was visiting me in New York, he went out to buy bagels. He returned carrying a paper bag full of ripe Comice pears. He peeled the tough skin from the fruit with his pocketknife, then fed the pears to me slice by slice, the juice running down his wrist.

When John left, I called Carol and told her I might be moving back to Boston.

8. Fania Kaplan

True to type, I had a psychotherapist. Her name was Fania Kaplan. I'd been seeing her for years. When I talked with Fania about John, I withheld the worrisome details. I told her about his job at MIT, his devotion to his daughters, his desire to have more children, how safe he made me feel. After each enumeration of his virtues, I added that John took really good care of himself. I said this so often that Fania grew suspicious and asked what I meant. That's when I told her that John was bipolar—that he had had a psychotic break fourteen years earlier, shortly after marrying Liz, and had been hospitalized for many months. (As a result of an odd coincidence, I had visited John in the hospital. I was traveling in Europe the summer after I graduated, and on my way back to my cheapie Paris hotel, I had bumped into John's brother and sister-in-law who were on holiday. They told me John was a patient at a Boston psychiatric hospital. When I returned home—this was before I moved to New York—I visited him there.)

Swimming laps in the hospital pool had helped John re-right his mood and get himself sprung from the hospital. Once home, he refused to take psychiatric meds, devoting himself instead to aerobic exercise—jogging, biking, swimming—and living an orderly life. (Regular habits and sufficient sleep are a big deal for people with mood disorders.) Slowly, courageously, John fought his way back to sanity. A psychiatric resident had told John's mother he would never do science again. With the support of his bosses, John white-knuckled his way back to the lab. Some years later John left Lincoln Labs for a job as a research scientist on the MIT campus in Cambridge, where he joined the university tae kwon do club, eventually earning a black belt. Tae kwon do channeled John's coiled—yet controlled—fury, helping him maintain his psychic balance.

Fania told me I had no idea what being married to a man with a chronic mental illness would be like. I decided to ignore her.

9. Hot Borscht

The first meal my future mother-in-law served me featured her homemade Latvian sourdough rye bread, hot borscht (beet soup made with meat and cabbage) and, for dessert, *panku-kas*, pancakes topped with sour cherry jam. The soup and the pankukas were secondary attractions; the rye bread was the heart and soul of the meal, and my response to it was a test of my suitability as a daughter-in-law.

10. Meeting Oma

It was cold and growing dark when John and I arrived at the door of his mother's overheated little unit in a housing complex for the elderly in Newton Centre. John knocked and we heard his mother's shuffling gait as she slowly approached the door. She faltered, unable to manipulate the latch. When the door finally opened, a small woman with keen eyes, a dark dress, and stockings rolled at the knees greeted us, speaking Latvian, a language unknown to me.

John gave his mother a cursory peck on her wrinkly cheek. She patted him, calling him Jāni. "Lovely to meet you," I said. Unsmiling, Oma watched me slip out of my heavy coat and boots.

We were going to a party later and I was wearing a print dress scattered with little flowers.

"Very nice," Oma said in heavily accented English.

There was not much to see in Oma's living room. Bare walls. A couch, a battered coffee table, a black-and-white television, a pair of unmatched chairs. Haphazardly dropped items of clothing. A child's American history primer in English. Books of Latvian poetry and folktales. A well-worn copy of Aleksandr Solzhenitsyn's *The Gulag Archipelago*—in the original Russian.

"Our party starts at seven, so we should eat," John said in English. He followed his mother into the kitchen to retrieve dishes, silver, glasses, and bits of paper towel to serve as napkins. I was directed toward the gray Formica table. I cleared a place for us to sit, pushing away bills, medicine bottles, a few curled photos, and a smudged glass candy dish containing broken-up pieces of Sky Bar. For the grandchildren.

The meal was ready. The food, except for the soup, was on the table, but before we could eat, John wanted to show me something. He dug around in his mother's crowded front closet. Eventually he returned to the table carrying a beaten-up white enamel bowl with a naked light bulb attached to it. By adding a heat source, John had transformed a vessel for soaking tired feet into a low-wattage bread dough incubator. Like a proud ten-year-old handing his mother a homemade birthday card, John showed off his creation.

"Jāni is very clever," Oma said. "And he is very practice, *praccal*," she added, reaching for the word but failing to find it. "Practical," I said, completing her thought, though in truth it was I who could not find words.

John served the borscht. To my surprise chunks of beef floated in the red, dill-flecked broth that Oma had topped with a spoonful of sour cream. (In my family, borscht was vegetarian beet soup served cold with a boiled potato and garnished with chopped dill.) The three of us contemplated our bowls, silently swirling the sour cream, watching carefully as the broth turned deep purplish pink. Oma and John stared at me as I buttered a slice of grayish brown rye bread—Oma's small electric oven was not hot enough to fully caramelize the rye, which would have darkened the bread inside and out. I sank my teeth into a slice.

"Firm," I said.

I sniffed.

"Caraway," I said.

"Sour and yet sweet," I said.

From their faces, I could see that I was on the right track. But more was expected.

"Mushroomy. Reminds me of the forest floor," I said.

I paused and then I did what I do when I don't know what else to do: I flattered. I gushed. I lied.

"This bread is a tour de force. A masterwork. A doorway into the past when poor people survived on bread alone. The staff of life. A religious experience," I said triumphantly. "What's in this bread?" I asked.

Now it was John's turn to talk. Thank Heavens.

He told me Oma's bread was made with whole-grain rye flour, salt, water, sourdough starter, sugar for flavor and contrast and to punch up the process of fermentation, a pinch of ground caraway, and, okay he'd admit it, a small amount of wheat flour to make the dough less sticky and easier to handle. The most authentic *rupjmaize* ("ruup-mize," the *j* is silent), he said, is made without wheat.

How long does it take to make this bread?

A day and a half.

"Oma kneads the bread herself," John added, "She's strong. Just look at her hands."

Oma interrupted, speaking in Latvian—translated by John—to tell me that when she was a little girl, her mother told her to knead the bread until sweat broke out on her forehead. When sweat appeared, the dough was ready for baking.

Now. Finally. We were allowed to eat.

"The rye bread is lovely with the soup," I said. "It has the same sour and sweet flavors going on. What a beautiful pairing . . ."

I praised and I flattered, but did I really like this rye bread with its tough crust and its sourish-sweetish interior?

No. Not really. Its color was an unappetizing gray. Nor did the tough texture and sauerkraut-y taste speak to my assimilated palate. A second-generation American, I had lost what the writer Saul Bellow called a "Litvak tongue," by which he meant a nostalgic longing for the sour flavors favored by Eastern Europeans, Jewish and gentile.

When we had taken our discussion of rye bread as far as it could go, we searched for common conversational ground and settled on the grandchildren—Oma had four. John's brother's son and daughter and John's daughters. No one mentioned the obvious—that John's brother was divorced, John was separated, and all four of her grandchildren were growing up in homes that did not include their fathers.

John rose to clear the table. We heard him in the kitchen, washing up. Oma asked me about my family. She wanted to know where my grandmother lived and who took care of her. This was not an idle question. Due to my mother's early marriage and Oma's late marriage, John's mother and my grandmother were more or less the same age. Did my grandmother live with my mother? Did my mother take care of her? Oma's real concern, though not addressed, was not unknown: She wanted to know if she would be invited to live with John and me when we married? I quickly changed the subject, telling Oma that I thought her Jāni was a wonderful father. So devoted to his girls. I wanted her to know how important this was to me.

"Jāni," Oma said firmly, delivering a timeless pronouncement, "has a very good char-*act*-ter," the emphasis on the middle syllable.

"Handsome too," I answered.

Oma silently gazed at me. I felt her taking in my face, my body, my being. When she spoke, she referred to my printed silk dress. "You will wear this dress when you attend the op-*per*-a with your husband," she said, again emphasizing the middle syllable. In these words, I heard her attachment to a world long lost—the glittering Riga opera—and something more: her wish that her son and I enjoy the best life has to offer. Thank you, I said, touched by her unexpected good wishes. (It did not occur to me that I was not the only flatterer in the room.)

John emerged from the kitchen. He and his mother spoke in Latvian. Then in English John said, "Our party starts soon. It's time to go." I rose, grabbed Oma's hands, and said I was looking forward to soon seeing her again. She looked in my eyes and said, "Jewish people are good family people."

11. I Pass the Test

Once outside, John and I kissed. Seemed I had passed the first test. That was good, but there would be more. We were on our way to a party at the Latvian social hall. There would be dancing and drinking and socializing with people nearly as old as my parents—John is only eight years older than I, but his Latvian friends were older than he, and our social worlds were out of whack, chronologically and otherwise. At the dance there would be many fair-haired people happily speaking Latvian, who would switch—or not switch—to English when I appeared. There would be a late supper featuring rye bread that, hungry or not, I'd feel obliged to consume. There would be more opportunities to explain that I lived in New York, but that I was planning to move to Newton. More chances to say that I, too, had roots in Eastern Europe. More occasions to state the obvious, that I was Jewish. More times to affirm that I truly, truly, loved rye bread.

12. Discriminations I Do Not Make

Driving to the dance, I had made a joke about spending Saturday night at a church social. If my friends knew where I was going, I said, I would lose my social standing as a member of New York's *hipoisie*. I had it wrong, John told me adamantly. We were not attending a church social. We were not attending a church anything. We were going to a party and dance at the Latvian social hall, a building untainted by Christian affiliation. So opposed was he to Christianity, John told me, that he refused to enter any church, including the Latvian Lutheran Church, even to attend a family event such as his nephew's confirmation.

"Funny," I said. "I'm Jewish. But I don't have a beef with Christianity."

"I do," said John.

13. Why John Called Himself a Pagan

Winners have the luxury of forgetting the past, but losers cling to the memory of their defeat for centuries. Millennia, even.

Roll the tape back eight hundred years . . .

In the twelfth and thirteen centuries, portions of modern-day Latvia and Estonia were forcibly Christianized during a series of German campaigns known as the Northern Crusades. John's ancestors lacked the invaders' sophisticated armory. To resist, they relied on guile. When the well-armed Crusaders rode into town demanding that the infidels convert to Christianity or face death, John's ancestors agreed with their fingers crossed behind their backs. They allowed themselves to be dunked in the Daugava River and baptized in exchange for the Germans building them a fortress, but when the German knights departed? They jumped back in the river and unbaptized themselves, so as not to offend their own more modest gods. Over time, however, might prevailed. The bitterness of forced conversion might have faded had the Crusaders been less greedy. While ostensibly saving souls, the Teutonic Knights staged a monumental land grab, seizing all the best land in Latvian provinces and elsewhere in the Baltic, and forcing the local population into servitude that lasted over seven hundred years.

14. There Was Another Reason

There were other reasons John called himself a pagan, by which he meant a follower of Latvia's pre-Christian religion. Not formally religious, he had a mystical, nature-worshipping streak. The antiauthoritarian pagan cosmology suited him. Moreover, he enjoyed getting a rise out of other people when he used the word. *Pagan*. It sounded so transgressive.

15. Exogamous Monogamous

At midnight, I was Cinderella in reverse: Happy to escape the ball. After the dance, John went to the men's room. I waited for him in the cloakroom. The scuffed wooden floors, the smell of ancient coal dust, the Ethan Frome desolation of the Latvian Center located in working-class Jamaica Plain made me homesick for my sparkly life in Manhattan. In my New York, creativity and breaking barriers—things I believed in—mattered more than anything. As did friendships with like-minded people who didn't necessarily have the same country of origin as you.

A tall woman, over forty, with a good figure, holding a poufy down coat, appeared in the cloakroom doorway. She addressed me in Latvian, then, noticing my incomprehension, she switched to English, asking me if I had seen a pair of black leather gloves with stitching on the front. I told her I had not. She paused and then stuck out her hand. "I'm Ilka," she said.

"Of course. You're a biologist, you live in Cambridge," I said, recalling the relief I'd felt earlier in the evening talking with another unmarried woman with a career.

"You went out with Jānis before he married Liz. I think we met at a concert," Ilga said.

"That was a long time ago," I said. "Fourteen years."

"I remember you," Ilka repeated. "You made Jānis laugh."

"I still do," I said, as the puzzle pieces in my head slowly rearranged themselves. She has a crush on him, I thought. And why wouldn't she? They're about the same age. He is attractive. She is attractive. He is unmarried. She is unmarried. Why shouldn't they find each other? Oh, of course. Of course. Now I get it. After divorcing his "American" wife, "Jānis" wasn't supposed to marry me, he was supposed to make up for his past mistake by marrying someone like Ilka. Someone Latvian. Certainly not American. And certainly, certainly, not a fast-talking Jewish person from New York City.

On our way back to Newton, the windshield wipers of John's superannuated International Harvester Travelall failing to keep up with the freezing slush outside the window, I told John about my encounter with Ilka and my realization that members of the exile community had their own ideas about whom he should choose as his second wife.

"I tried," he said with a sigh. "Maija Ozols. Ivars introduced us and I dated her when Liz and I separated. She's a pediatrician . . . a few years younger than you. Intelligent. I liked her. She was here tonight, but you might not have noticed her."

"Not flashy enough for you?" I asked.

"It wasn't that," John said. "She's attractive . . . Good company too. There just wasn't a spark. Her grandmother was a friend of Oma's. When I thought about having sex with her, I would imagine those two old ladies sitting in the corner of the bedroom, rubbing their hands together, watching us. I couldn't do it. I tried. She tried too. But nothing."

"You are the ultimate exogamous monogamous," I said.

"What do you mean?" John asked.

"You can only mate and marry outside your group."

John quickly made a connection between my remark and the sentiment expressed in many of the traditional Latvian poems called *dainas*, noting that "The dainas say a man should saddle his horse and ride far away in search of a wife. There's wisdom in that. And not just because of the gene pool . . ."

"Aha," I said. "But do the dainas tell a man to saddle his horse and ride three hundred miles south, crossing borders and rivers and not stopping until he arrives in Slutsk, the Jewish shtetl in Belarus where his future wife's Bubbe spent her first nine years?"

16. Dainas 1

The dainas that John loved so much and quoted so often are four-line poems (often sung; often referred to as folk songs) that describe the life cycle of Latvian peasants. The seasons passing. Young people marrying. Old people dying. Some dainas are hundreds of years old. Some are thought to be much, much older, although scholars find it difficult to assign dates since no one systematically wrote down the lyrics until the end of the nineteenth century. That's when a generation of young rebels began thinking about dainas as "vehicles of memory" expressing their hunger for political autonomy. (One scholar explained the historical importance of the dainas, writing that "folklore served to create a national consciousness and pride." This sentiment helped fuel the Latvian independence movement.)

The hero of this movement, Krišjānis Barons, in the hope of instilling pride in the hearts of his countrymen, helped launch a campaign to collect, study, and eventually publish folk song lyrics. Barons appealed to women in rural areas, asking for their help in particular, because it was they who led the singing of folk songs during seasonal celebrations and it was they who most cherished these short verses in which so much meaning was enfolded. Some of these women told Barons that they had learned to properly read and write in order to help him compile a catalogue of the dainas.

Thousands of correspondents, men as well as women, sent Barons over a quarter of a million of these short poems. Today, there are over a million on file at the National Library in Riga. Barons believed the folk songs expressed the spiritual beliefs of the Latvian people. They are, he wrote, "the vessels of their soul."

17. Dainas 2

Some non-Latvian scholars who have studied the dainas expressed astonishment at their beauty and moral sophistication. One opined that these poems possessed a beauty more splendid than anything in Western canon except the early songs of the Greek Islanders. The dainas, this scholar wrote, were "written at the morning of the world, and the dew is still on them."

18. Dainas 3

Two folk songs describing rye cultivation and rye bread were among John's favorites. The first, which describes Dievs, the ancient Baltic god, striding through a field of rye, seems like one of the very old ones. (Some experts believe the dainas are related to the Hindu vedas, a literary tradition that originated eight thousand years ago.) The Dievs daina described in symbolic terms the time when rye, a fast-replicating grass that evolved in the Middle East, spread across northeastern Europe. This event occurred thousands of years before the first veda was composed. The song makes more sense when you know that rye turns a warm, earthy gray color when it is ready to be harvested:

> Dievs was striding through the rye field
> He was wearing a gray coat
> When he reached the edge he spread
> Over it gray ears of rye

The second rye daina John loved was very different from the first. This verse was homey. Earnest. Highly domesticated. And prayerful in a way that recalled Christianity, whether it was Christian or not. Though Lutheranism has been the established religion in Latvia for five hundred years, many Latvians, Christian and non-, cling to pagan ideas and a mystical understanding of the natural world:

> God grant that I should die
> As did Father, as did Mother
> Father—threshing in the barn,
> Mother—kneading dough for bread

This daina seems to have comforted Krišjānis Barons, because he recited it over and over in the months before his death. At the end of his life, Barons said he wanted no monument to be erected—he wanted the dainas to be his sole memorial.

19. Carriage House

"Latvians are as bound to place . . . as other peoples are bound to tribal legend . . ."

—E. V. Bunkše

During his "brief bachelorhood" (that's how John describes the time between breaking up with Liz and getting serious with me), John lived in a nineteenth-century wood-framed carriage house located conveniently near his old house, where his daughters lived with their mom and stepfather-to-be. John loved this little house and when he described it, it sounded so romantic. But when I stayed there with him for a week while researching an article, I was shocked. The carriage house, I joked, was a rebuke to romantic illusions: dank rather than cozy, with stained turquoise wall-to-wall carpet, mold blooming in the prefab shower, and a kitchen sink barely big enough to wash your hands in. John didn't see it that way. He liked living in a little house that was old and dark and made of wood. A house with history, where harnesses were repaired and horse-drawn carriages were polished. I didn't understand when he told me he felt safe in his small, dear home. I didn't understand when he told me that when he moved into the carriage house, having left his family behind, he would lie in bed at night in that creaking wooden house and sing folk songs to drive away his sadness.

20. Molly Bloom

Since the kitchen could not accommodate us both working at the same time, I stood and watched as John put salted water up to boil, then scrubbed and quartered Yukon gold potatoes. He sharpened his chef's knife, then sliced cucumbers and chopped fresh dill for a salad he later doused with sour cream. He removed from its paper wrapping the cod he'd bought on the way home from work and held it up for inspection. The fish glistened as fresh fish does. He ran it under the faucet in cold water, patted it dry with paper towels, and cut it into portions. He dredged each piece of fish twice—first in beaten egg, then in breadcrumbs. When the girls arrived, red-cheeked from the cold—they'd ridden their bikes from their mom's house to his—he fried the fish in butter. So much butter. His display of paternal generosity turned me into Molly Bloom reciting a silent soliloquy. And yes, I said yes I will leave New York and marry you. Yes, I will. Yes. A new kind of desire took root inside me at that moment, flowering in the loamy soil of John's generosity and his paternal devotion.

21. The Girls

As John fried the fish, the girls and I went looking for placemats, napkins, dishes, silverware, and glasses. Four of each. Ilze, thirteen, yanked open an overstuffed drawer in the only closet in the house. Head down, butt up in the air, she began taking things out of the bottom drawer. A clear plastic shower curtain. Three white terry washcloths. A tea cozy. Navy blue running shorts.

"I found them," she announced triumphantly, holding up four woven mats.

"From my dowry," John explained from his spot in front of the stove—meaning Liz had given him these housewares when he moved out.

"Where are the napkins?" I asked.

"No napkins. Not necessary," John said.

"Of course we need napkins," I said, as Ilze, whose bustling competence seemed at odds with her prepubescent frame, dug out four almost-new yellow cotton napkins.

"More stuff from Mom," she said.

"Do you think there's a bathmat in there?" I asked.

"You could use this on the floor?" Ilze said, pulling out a raggedy blue towel.

John looked up. "That towel traveled all over Europe with me. It went camping on the French Riviera . . ."

"Maybe it deserves a decent burial," I said, playing to the girls.

Sarma, who was nine and elfin, filled the water glasses from the tap and we sat down. John opened a bottle of Italian white using the corkscrew on his Swiss Army knife. As he poured the wine, I asked the girls about their day. My presence gave them a free pass to speak English—usually with their dad they spoke Latvian, a language that had an inhibiting impact on their conversation.

Sarma complained about her art teacher.

"Jessie doesn't like him," she said, referring to her best friend. "She told him real artists don't follow directions."

"What do you think?" I asked.

"I like making pictures," Sarma said. She paused. "The art teacher wears shoes that look like horseshoe crabs only without the antenna."

"Most men teachers dress funny," Ilze chimed in. "Mr. Garrett doesn't, though. He wears black turtlenecks with corduroy pants and cool-looking black shoes."

When we finished eating, Sarma, an oversized workman's cap covering her dirty blonde curls, climbed onto John's lap.

"You need to trim your ogre hairs," she said, yanking lightly on John's bushy eyebrows.

"And your droopy mustache," Ilze added.

Sarma ran her hand over John's cheek. "You missed a spot," she said.

John played along as the girls deconstructed his grooming and wardrobe, saving their worst disdain for the grotty yellow windbreaker he wore while biking to work. And as far as his white plastic safety helmet was concerned . . .

"You look like you're wearing half a soccer ball on your head," Ilze said.

Sarma wanted to know if he was going to attach a square mirror to his bicycle helmet, "Like the ones at the dentist?"

I told the girls I had recently met Oma and tasted her famous rye bread.

Ilze was of the opinion that *rupjmaize* is good, but not for school lunches. "The worst thing is when he makes us lunch," Ilze said pointing to her dad. "Cottage cheese and rye bread sandwiches. Yuck. No cookies. No chips. Just an apple. Last week a kid stole my lunch bag out of my locker. I found it in the girls' bathroom. Nothing had been taken."

"My mom eats peanut butter, cottage cheese, and jam on rye bread. She calls that her power breakfast," Sarma said, jumping off of John's lap. She opened the front door, stuck her bottom into the cold February air, and stood there for a moment.

"Pass gas," she said by way of explanation, after slamming the door shut and returning to the table.

She climbed back on John's lap. "What do you call a person who doesn't fart in public?" she asked.

Answer: A private tutor.

"What is it called when the Queen of England farts?" she asked.

Answer: A noble gas.

"What's in space, has feathers, and goes 'fart, fart, fart?'"

Answer: UFO. Unidentified Farting Ostrich.

"Where'd you get all these?" I asked.

"I got a kids' joke book in the Nashville airport last week," Sarma said.

Everyone was silent for a moment as we considered the luxe life the girls were living with their mom and stepdad-to-be, who owned a company and flew his own airplane.

"I've got a joke," John said after a moment.

Why was the lamb punished?

Answer: Because he was *baaaaaaad* . . .

"But that's not a fart joke," Sarma told him.

Soon it was time to go. It was dark. John would drive his daughters home, throwing their bikes in the back of his TravelAll. As the girls gathered up their belongings and slipped into their down jackets, we made plans to get together on Sunday for brunch. I offered to make French toast with maple syrup—"There's more to life than rye bread," I said. John made a face. "It's okay," I said, patting his shoulder. "We can make applesauce to go with the French toast."

I was washing the dishes when John returned. He nuzzled his cold face against my neck. "The girls love you," he said.

"Well, I love them too," I said, knowing now I was in this thing for keeps.

22. Scarlet O'Hara

I told the only woman I knew in Boston—she was a culinary historian and understood my preoccupation with food—that I was marrying John because with him, I would never go hungry. I meant it as a joke, although it wasn't a joke. I understood it as a metaphor, although it wasn't a metaphor—it was what you get when fact and metaphor are kneaded together and left to rise.

23. John Liked Everything About Me

With John, there was no "if only" clause attached to compliments. He didn't think I needed to contain myself. He didn't think I should lose five pounds or ten. He liked my big bones. What a relief to be appreciated for what I was, who I was. As to the women on magazine covers, the slender, elusive ones, John wasn't impressed. "Nice face," he'd say, "but *tooooo* skinny."

24. A Second Wife Is Not a Bride

In June 1982, I sublet my apartment on West Eighty-fourth Street and traveled north to Boston with two large suitcases, my electric typewriter, and a bunch of books and notebooks. Since there was no place in the carriage house for me to work, I rented a room in a Cambridge boarding house. We bought a second car, a standard-shift yellow Subaru station wagon that was easier to drive than John's TravelAll.

Arriving back at the carriage house one evening, I parked the Subaru on the drive next to a familiar forest green Range Rover. Inside I found Liz sitting at the table with John. She had brought over their divorce papers to be signed. The two of them were holding hands, and they were both crying. They barely acknowledged me.

I went into the bedroom and closed the door. I had given up New York for this guy, and he hadn't even made room for me in the closet when I moved in. And now this.

Later when I told John how uncomfortable I felt walking in on this scene, he did not apologize or even respond to how I felt.

"We were married for thirteen years," he said. "It's sad. She's the mother of my children . . ."

25. Goodbye Carriage House

In the fall we moved into an apartment on the top floor of a house located within walking distance of Newton Centre. Our new home came equipped with the essentials—numerous closets, a kitchen large enough to accommodate a table, a bathroom equipped with a bathtub, and two reasonably sized bedrooms (one for the girls). Our plan was to buy a house in the spring. In the meantime, I had a mold-free place to hang my hat. And my coat. And my favorite black pants.

26. Wedding 1 (November 1982)

Driving to our wedding in our new yellow Subaru, John said something that surprised me. "In my first marriage, I did all the giving," he said. With me, it was different. "You do all the giving."

What he said wasn't true. But it was scary.

27. Wedding 2

We were married in Cambridge, Massachusetts, on a cold, sunny Sunday afternoon in November, in a drawing room owned by Harvard University that we sexed up with pots of red and hot-pink cyclamen.

A federal judge officiated. In his remarks he described John and me as "two peas in a pod," a comment that I long pondered. He concluded his remarks by saying that John's and my relationship "was the envy of all those present." He did not refer to our religions or ethnicities. Which doesn't mean these subjects were not present in the room.

At the reception my family and my friends from New York sat on one side of the room. John's family and the members of his folklore group sat on the other. John and I sat in the middle with Ilze and Sarma. Our ersatz family of four was an island of neutrality, our own little Switzerland. Inside this unit, where one would most expect divided loyalties to fester, we four had made a home.

After lunch the band played "Hava Nagila," an Israeli folk song (based on a Ukrainian melody) exhorting Jews to rejoice in their nationhood. My friends and family, plus John, danced the hora. Then the Latvians rose to sing two folk songs expressing, in code, their country's yearning for nationhood. John left my side to join in the singing. I stayed where I was. No one on *his* side explained what the songs were about or translated the lyrics. No one on *my* side—certainly not I—asked them to. All seemed content to remain segregated.

Sometime during the festivities one of my uncles cornered my new husband to tell him that many Latvians were "Jew killers." Then a small-eyed red-haired woman from the Latvian side of the room stopped me on my way to the ladies' room to tell me that our wedding was, "Just nothing. Neither Latvian, nor Jewish." I guess she found the kosher corned beef insufficiently ethnic, though my mother had purchased this slab of meat and given it to the caterer in hopes of adding American-style Yiddishkeit to the buffet table. And why, the aggrieved guest continued, was there no Latvian rye bread accompanying the corned beef?

After John and I cut the chocolate wedding cake, Carol toasted our marriage, as did some of my other New York friends. John's brother gave a brief toast and then Ilze, not yet fourteen, saluted John and me, praising her father's fine qualities as a father and celebrating the happiness I had brought their family. So touched was I by Ilze's words, I didn't notice that none of John's friends had anything good to say about our union.

28. Honeymoon

Our honeymoon was a three-week quasi-business trip spent visiting John's friends and collaborators in Switzerland, Germany, Italy, and France. John's preferred method of European transport was a rental car, and we kept the same white Volkswagen diesel the whole time we were away. John took as many pictures of the car as he took of me.

I had dreaded traveling in Germany, but found myself charmed by a country where families hiked together on Sunday afternoon, after which they drank coffee and ate apple cake. It helped that John's friends treated me like visiting royalty. In Stuttgart, we stayed with Gert and Gerta, architects married to one another, whom John had met as a young postdoc working in that city. Like John, Gert and Gerta were small children during the war.

Watching John in their kitchen, I was able to locate John's odd domestic habits: the unsliced bread left cut side down on the bread board. The leftovers covered by an upside-down glass bowl. The whole-grain crackers and fine jam. The wildflowers in little pots. The open windows and heavy cotton sheets. The little slivers of soap that were never thrown out.

John's habits belonged to this place, this country where quality materials and small artistic gestures were treasured and past privations were never far from mind.

29. Egg

From Stuttgart we drove south to Egg, the hamlet in south-west Germany where John lived for five years as a child. We motored up a hill, took a sharp turn off a paved road, and drove past a handwritten sign. And there it was. A dozen weary stucco farmsteads, strung out along a dirt road, which had once been surrounded by fields and were now surrounded by orchards.

Morning mist rose up from withered grass. Behind a scrim of white, we saw the black trunks and leafless twisty limbs of fruit trees. The outline of large, unidentifiable beasts loomed in the mist. Horses. Thoroughbreds standing still on slender legs among the trees, heads turned in our direction. The silent village, the vaporous white light, the now-you-see-me-now-you-don't trickery of horses hidden among trees, the scene was opaque, ungraspable. I shivered.

John wanted to walk through the woods to the nearby village of Ebenweiler, where he had spent a great deal of time as a child. (No other refugees lived in Egg, but many lived in Ebenweiler.) "Come on," he said, grabbing my hand, and then he stopped. "Your hands are cold," he said.

"I left my gloves in the car."

"You can wear mine. Or we can share," John said, linking his right arm with my left and handing me a single glove. "Stick your other hand in your pocket to keep it warm, and I'll do the same."

We *swish swish*ed our way through a carpet of dried leaves.

"The woods are so German," I said. "Scary clean."

"In Germany anyone can collect firewood off the forest floor. It doesn't matter who owns the land. People carry out the deadwood. So the woods are always clean."

"Too clean," I said. "Too German."

"I spent a lot of time here climbing the tallest trees. Barefoot."

"Barefoot?"

"Kids went barefoot from April to October."

"Weren't you cold?"

"Just my feet. My feet were always cold. Shoes were too precious to wear. I had an old pair of boots. I think they must have been my brother's. But they had holes. Oma put cardboard in them, which was useless because of the snow."

We walked in silence down an incline through a dense grove of pines where little light penetrated.

"Oma sent me here to collect firewood at night."

"Spooky," I said. "Weren't you scared?"

"Of the wild boars, yes, they're vicious, but not of the dark. Your eyes adjust to darkness and most nights you have the moon. What's really scary is the stuff you imagine.

"Once my friend Marģeris and I found a dead body in the woods. He'd killed himself," John said, pausing to take a deep breath. "The dead guy was this kid, maybe nineteen years old, who'd been conscripted into the Latvian Legion to fight against the Russians on the Eastern Front. He was attending the Latvian high school in Ebenweiler. His leg had been shot off during the war and he had shrapnel in his head. He had terrible headaches. And he was alone. No one knew what had happened to his family. Probably they were dead."

I look at John. His face was expressionless.

"I remember hearing the grownups talk about this guy. People in the Latvian camp knew he was in a bad way, but nobody knew what to do.

"Then he went missing. Everyone searched for him. The lake in Ebenweiler where we swam, I will show it to you when we get there, the lake was dredged, but his body was never found. . . . It was creepy thinking he was out there. . . . When I swam, if my leg touched something under the water, I'd jump, thinking it was him trying to drag me down. To this day, I get spooked when my head is underwater and I can't see and a bit of grass grabs at my leg."

"Then what happened?"

"About a year after he went missing, a woman from the village was hunting for mushrooms and strayed pretty far from the path. She crawled into a dense stand of young pines on her hands and knees. What she saw terrified her. She took one look and ran back to the village.

"Marģeris, my friend from Latvian school, and I heard that a body had been found in a thicket of fir trees. We knew right away where that was. We raced to the woods. We wanted to be the first to see the dead guy. But we were little kids. As we approached the thicket we heard something moving in the underbrush. Probably an animal rattling a branch. We jumped. We looked at each other and then we raced back down to the lake, where a bunch of the older kids were playing. We told them we knew where the body was. We led them back to the spot and then on all fours we followed them into the clearing." John paused. His face, still expressionless.

"The guy had used his belt to hang himself from a small tree. One vertebra was still hanging from his belt. The rest of his bones had been carried off by animals. One of his boots contained decomposing human flesh. It smelled like a dead animal. Nothing else remained of him except for his wallet containing worthless old Reichsmarks. He killed himself before the currency revaluation. . . . That was in 1948, I think."

"Like a scene from a horror movie," I said.

"I hate horror movies," John said.

"I do too . . ."

"Do you notice," John said after a while, "Our strides are similar. We walk in step, even though I'm taller."

"My legs are long. I guess that's why it works," I said.

"What matters is that it works," John said, squeezing my arm.

I didn't know if he was right. I loved John. I was drawn to him, but he bewildered me.

Where did he hide his emotions?

30. Totemic Speech

How many times over the years have I heard the story about him and Marģeris finding that body? Ten times? One hundred times? More? Early in our marriage I began to sense some invocation of magic in John's need to tell his stories again and again. As if each story enfolded realms of hidden meaning. Totemic Speech, I called John's way of invoking the past.

31. The Oft-Repeated, Never-Processed Past

Maybe I am writing this book to accomplish what John has not. Process the past, so that he might be less encumbered.

32. The Cost of War

We drove to Italy through the Alps, spending the weekend in the South Tyrolean town of Bressanone—in German, the name was Brixen. (Both Italy and Austria claimed naming rights over this long-contested area.) Hiking on Saturday morning, we stopped to peer into a tiny one-room church perched on a hillside. A fenced churchyard crowded with gravestones surrounded the dollhouse-sized structure. Adorning the church wall were four small memorial photographs reproduced in porcelain. Regarding this wall, John's and my memories differ slightly. What we both remember: The photos captured the images of four young men with the same last name, probably brothers, dressed in German uniforms. Studying the photos and the family inscriptions, we realized each brother had been killed in a different World War II battle. John and I stood together, silently contemplating these lost children. You see so many things when traveling. You never know what will stick. But this memorial to the wartime tragedy of just one family remained with us, with both of us, becoming in time one of the shared memories that defines our marriage.

33. Dolomites

The sun had disappeared. The hills were gray. The air was cold and damp and very smelly. Preparing for winter, farmers in the South Tyrol had chosen the Saturday of our visit to pump the animal waste they'd been collecting all summer and fall into the special tanks they used to fertilize their fields. The odor of ammonia—and worse—filled our noses as we lay on a high hillside watching tractors outfitted with these tanks scurrying like ants back and forth, spraying organic waste on denuded fields. How comic and yet unsettling that this was the place we chose to decide the ethnic and religious identities of the children we hoped to have. How odd, too, to remember how blithely we made these decisions.

John told me he felt personally responsible for the survival of Latvia's language and its culture, both of which were under attack from the Soviet Union. Above all, it was important to him that our future children, like his daughters, speak Latvian. As long as they were not Christian, he didn't care what religion they embraced. For my part, though I was only casually observant, I wanted our children to be Jewish and possess what I did not: sufficient background in Hebrew to become bar or bat mitzvah and find a place for themselves in the stream of Jewish history.

Sitting on our backpacks to keep our bottoms dry, we decided our offspring would be Latvian-speaking Jews. John would "get" ethnicity and language and I would "get" religion and that was that. But, of course, that was not that. You cannot divvy up what is not divisible. Allegiance. Identity. The inner recesses of the human heart.

We conceived our son, my only birth child, on that trip. I like to think we made our baby in Italy, but his conception could have taken place on the German side of the mountains.

34. Reject! Reject!
One winter afternoon, pregnant belly out to here, I raced into the Star Market in Newtonville to pick up a few things for

dinner. The Latvian woman who had described our wedding as "just nothing" accosted me in the vegetable aisle to ask how my Latvian language lessons were progressing. I reacted to this question as if I my body were being forced to accept nonautologous blood. My immune system shouted Reject! REJECT! I informed her that I was not learning to speak Latvian, but that John's study of Yiddish was coming along well.

I didn't get it. The way people in the Latvian exile community had so many thoughts and opinions about how I should live, when they didn't even know me. On the airplane returning home from our honeymoon, I had written thank-you notes to all the members of John's folklore group; long, gracious notes (I was a writer, after all) thanking them for the painting they had given us as a wedding gift—it was quite an accomplished painting. I had stamped and mailed the letters when we got home from Europe and that was that. A few weeks after bumping into the first disapproving Latvian woman, I ran into someone else, another Latvian woman, who asked why I had failed to thank so and so, adding that I had hurt so and so's feelings. I explained that it was not my intention to snub anyone. John had given me the list of people to be thanked and I had gone down the list checking off one name after another. Any oversight was completely inadvertent. I went home and wrote another thank-you note, this one apologizing for the delay and then expressing my thanks. After mailing the note, I couldn't stop thinking about the fact that this mistake had been a topic of conversation. That a simple oversight had been dissected and then interpreted as a deliberate insult.

This animus came as a shock to me. I was used to being liked. I was not a "groupy" person, but in New York I had lots of friends who loved me. I loved them, too. The fact that a pre-selected group gossiped about me and assumed the worst about me gave me the creeps.

I shut down. These were not my people. I wasn't going to make an effort.

And, for the most part, I did not.

35. I Called Him John

His family called him Jāni. Members of the Latvian community called him Jānis. I tried calling him Yanni, but that name felt contrived. Fifteen years before, when we'd met, he'd introduced himself to me as John. His first wife called him John. His colleagues at MIT—the first friends we made together—called him John. So I called him John, although using that bland moniker jabbed at me. Just as he was alienated from his name in English, so was I.

36. What Did John's Love Look Like?

I was pregnant and we were worried about money, so I bought a cheap maternity dress, brown with a big white acetate bow at the neck. I tried the dress on for John and he told me to return it and buy something better. So I did.

37. Newton Bathtub

One Saturday night in February, I climbed into the bathtub and announced to John that I planned to stay there. Maybe forever. Consequently, I would not be able to accompany him to the concert and social gathering at the Latvian hall later that evening. Submersion seemed my best response to a life that had careened off course. How else was I to understand how a city girl such as I had landed in Newton, Massachusetts, with boobs as ginormous as the balloons in the Macy's Thanksgiving Day parade, contemplating a Saturday evening listening to music I did not care for, amidst people who did not think I was funny or winning or even worthy. Clearly my locomotive had jumped its track. Until I came up with a better solution, I would remain here in this soothing warm water that I could refill and reheat at will.

When darkness began to fall, John returned to the bathroom. He stood next to the tub, looking down on my large white form.

"But what are you going to do about supper?" he asked.

"I don't know and I don't care" was my highly evolved answer.

"You need to eat," he said.

John left the bathroom. I heard him in the kitchen. A short time later he returned carrying the leaf from the birch table I had brought with me from New York. He placed the board lengthwise across the tub, creating a kind of breakfast-in-bed tray for the bathtub. He returned with silverware, a glass, and a napkin, and a plate laden with scrambled eggs, sliced tomatoes, buttered rye bread, and a small pot of jam.

I looked at the food.

I said nothing.

What was I to do?

I dug into supper, putting jam on the bread, downing the eggs. I ate everything on my plate. Still I said nothing.

John ate his eggs and rye bread in the kitchen with only Garrison Keillor to keep him company. Then he returned to the bathroom. He looked at me. Without saying a word, he offered me his hand. I took his hand and stepped out of the tub. I went into the bedroom, donned my stylish maternity dress, the one John had urged me to buy, and a bright red necklace that I hoped would serve as a diversion from the broad expanse of my chest, and I went with John to the Latvian social hall. I could not understand a word of what was said or sung. And I really wasn't welcome. But a few people made what felt like a genuine effort—I was grateful for that—and I made an effort, too. Mostly, though, I was there. Present. John's wife.

John's kindness had shamed me into doing the right thing.

And equally to the point: we had found our way to one of the cardinal rules of our marriage. Misbehavior would remain at home. In public, we would present a united front.

38. His Secrets

We were recently married. Noah was not yet born. We were sitting at the dining room table after dinner. I asked John about his breakdown, knowing I was transgressing.

At first, he was silent. Then he said, "I hate that expression. Nothing broke."

"You were in the hospital. I visited you there," I said.

The dining room was dim. John's face was in shadows.

"What was it like?" I asked. It was my right to know, wasn't it? Weren't married people supposed to tell each other everything?

"I spit in their faces." John said.

"Whose faces?" I asked.

But that's all he would say.

In time he told me more, but only bits and pieces, details like shards of glass from a shattered mosaic. But there was no heartfelt discussion. These memories were his and I should stay out of it.

It was the same with his nightmares. Every few months he woke in the night moaning and crying out. Sensing his thrashing in my sleep, I would wake. Turning toward him, leaning against him, I would tell him, "It's only a dream. It's only a dream." I would repeat those words until the thrashing stopped and the crying out stilled, and he fell back to sleep. In the morning he would not tell me what he'd dreamt.

39. Married Love

Before I was too pregnant to travel, I planned one last visit to New York, to meet with magazine editors, to spend time with my friends, and to reimmerse in the intensity of the urban visual. (Bruegel on Hudson. All the world crammed onto one tiny island. How I missed it.)

My flight departed at 11 a.m. on a Saturday in early June.

I was staying with my friend Lara in Tribeca. My plan was to take a cab to Lara's, freshen up, and then the two of us would go to dinner and the theater—Lara, who was almost old enough to be my mother, had gotten tickets for us to see Tommy Tune's revival of the Gershwins' *My One and Only*.

Weather delayed the flight from Logan to LaGuardia. The takeoff was okay, but ten minutes in, the wild rumpus began. The plane bounced up and down; and then without warning, it dropped one hundred, two hundred, maybe three hundred feet. Like an untethered elevator careening toward concrete. A few people screamed. A woman moaned. The contents of my stomach rose. I grabbed the hand of the man sitting next to me. My brain congealed around the thought of my unborn child. My baby. My baby. My baby. My baby. He must not die. I gagged, swallowed and gagged again reaching for the puke bag.

And then the plane righted itself.

Everyone exhaled in unison . . .

And waited for the next jolt.

Nothing happened.

"Ladies and Gentlemen. Seems like we hit an itty-bitty air pocket," announced the pilot through a scrim of static. Folksy as hell. Not a smidge of emotion. Just us hayseeds out for a little airplane ride.

Waves of adrenaline fueled by a wild impulse to protect my unborn child swept through my body. I understood that I would die for this baby, I would claw the face of anyone who threatened him.

To calm myself, I closed my eyes and imagined John's body. His chest. His shoulders. All my favorite parts. I was seven months pregnant and I was in love with my husband's body. I had never before lost myself like this. John's body was my home. My bower. My safe place on earth. Our bed was the center of the universe. Not just because of the sex—though hormone-fueled, urgent yet awkward pregnancy sex was a revelation. What blew my mind was the mammalian attachment. The meter never ran out on our holding, hugging, and snuggling. At every opportunity—Sunday mornings were the best—we lay in bed encircled in each other's arms, skin to skin, talking and laughing. My husband, my Johnny, he of the fearsome eyebrows, the Prussian posture, the militantly unsmiling face, had a puppy dog's hunger for affection.

Was this the mystery enfolded in marriage?

Did all husbands and wives dwell at night in this secret garden?

The pilot came on to tell us that twenty-seven flights were stacked up before us waiting to land at LaGuardia. We would have to circle the airport until it was our turn to land.

Circle. And circle. And circle. The plane rising and dipping in its orbit, the bile in my gullet rising and dipping, too.

I arrived frazzled and nauseous at Lara's apartment. Dinner would have to wait if we were going to make it to the theater on time. Knowing I needed to eat, Lara made me a chicken sandwich. I can't remember how it was decided that I needed a bath to restore my composure. What I remember is standing in Lara's bathroom admiring the beauty of the space, its cleanliness and tranquility. Lara turned on the spigots. Hot, steamy water cascaded into the tub as I stripped off all my clothes, the cotton undies, the embarrassing pregnancy bra, the red necklace, everything. Before plunging into the water, I turned to show Lara my belly, my watermelon breasts. All my adult life, I had preferred being naked with men. Men were so forgiving. So grateful for female generosity. Women were different. The way they eyed each other in the locker room, weighing and assessing, searching for imperfection. But judgment could not touch me. Today I stood upright in the bathtub proclaiming my presence on this earth as assertively as one of those squat Paleolithic fertility goddesses. The ones with the huge bellies and vastly pendulous breasts. I was married. I was pregnant. I was unashamed.

40. Married Hatred

(This incident occurred at the summer solstice celebration at Piesaule, the Latvian camp in New Hampshire, in late June, seven months after we started seeing each other again, four months before we were married. I am placing it here, following my tale of married love, because this is where it belongs.)

We were running late and John was antsy.

We had pulled off the highway and climbed a hill to pick wildflowers. It took a while, as the girls needed to make wreaths for their hair and for mine, too. That was the mid-summer tradition. All that flower-picking and wreath-making took time. It was nearly five when we exited the highway onto a dirt road snaking along the lake and back into the woods. At the camp entrance, John stopped to pay. Wreaths atop their heads, the girls jumped out of the car and raced off to find their friends. We drove down the dirt road to Zane Rosental's cabin, where the members of John's folklore group, the group he helped found a dozen years before, were gathering.

Zane's house was built on the side of a typical New Hampshire hillside—lots of granite and scrubby pines. There was no driveway. You parked your car at the bottom and climbed up a steep walkway. It had rained heavily the week before and the runoff had cut deep, intermittent ditches along the side of the narrow road. To park, you needed to cozy up to the side of the hill, leaving room for other cars to pass, while avoiding the troughs where the road was washed out. This was tricky.

John told me to get out of the car and direct him as he backed the car into a small dry area flat against the hill located between two ditches.

I was a left-handed New Yorker—not spatially talented to begin with—who didn't own a car. Who hadn't driven much in nearly fifteen years. I tried to tell John that I might not be the right person for the job. But he didn't listen. Liz was good at driving and spatial stuff, so I must be, too. I got out of the car and stood in the middle of the dirt road, flapping my arms up and down, like a distressed bird. I had no idea what I was supposed to do.

"Come this way," I said without conviction, my words punctuated with more arm flapping.

John stepped on the accelerator, and the brand-new Subaru wagon lurched into a ditch that was at least a foot deep. John jiggled the gearshift, moving from front wheel to four-wheel drive. He stepped on the gas pedal, and the wheels whirred and whirred again, digging him deeper and deeper into the mud.

"You were supposed to help me," John hissed. The fury in his eyes shocked me. "You are supposed to be on my side," he said. There was no humor, no love, no emotion that I recognized in his voice or on his face.

"I am on your side," I insisted, "I just don't understand what you want me to do."

"You were supposed to help me park the car," John repeated angrily, as if he were a heart surgeon, and I, the stupid nurse who had just dropped the scalpel.

It was an epochal moment. The rage and dismissal on John's face were seared into my consciousness.

We weren't married yet.

I didn't have a name for what I was experiencing. I had no idea how to categorize the cold-eyed, hot-hearted judgment in John's eyes. Eighteen months later, when I was married, with a tiny baby, and struggling to adjust to my new life in Boston, I thought about this incident. By then I could name what I had seen in John's eye. It was marital hatred. The flame that ignites in your heart when you experience the person you are closest to on earth as your worst enemy.

Eventually, a guy with a truck and industrial-weight chains pulled the Subaru out of the ditch and we climbed the hill to the party.

We never discussed what had happened; but silence did not erase the memory. Forever after that, I associated Midsummer Festival—John's favorite holiday—as the day I learned that love is only one end of the marital emotional continuum.

41. Marriage: Second Definition

Marriage: An intimate relationship existing on a continuum

between love and hate, with partners perpetually suspended between the two.

42. Feeding Noah

The weather was warm. The windows were wide open. Afternoon light poured into the kitchen and was absorbed by the dark-stained woodwork surrounding the windows.

Noah was eleven months old. Getting ready to walk. Like a chortling sumo wrestler, he stood in front of the under-counter spice cabinet, stacking and sorting glass jars of cinnamon and ground ginger, bay leaf, cumin, black peppercorns, and dill weed.

At 5 p.m. I scooped him up and sat him in his high chair. I slipped the tray into place and locked it. Suppertime. On the tray, I placed a bit of rye bread smeared with peanut butter. He picked up the slice and happily gnawed it. Then I placed a small piece of filet of sole I had just sautéed and let cool, plus soft steamed broccoli florets in front of him. I watched as he smashed fistfuls of fish and veg into his avid little mouth. Last course: a plastic cup filled with sweet-potato puree. Sweet-potato mash went everywhere—into his mouth, yes, but also onto his face. His eyelashes. Spikey strands of orange hair sprang from his head. Still I didn't intervene. Why shouldn't he enjoy himself? Bath time was next.

Oma, who still lived in her subsidized apartment in Newton Centre, was visiting. She had been sunning herself in our back-yard. She entered the kitchen as I lifted Noah into his highchair.

Silently she watched her grandson enjoy his tactile meal.

When he began to finger paint with the leftovers, Oma moved in on him with a spoon in her hand saying "Eat. Eat. Eat. Eat." Only she said it in Latvian: *"Ed. Ed. Ed. Ed."*

"Oma," I said, "For God's sake, leave him alone."

Fumbling to unlatch the high hair tray, I lifted Noah into my arms on our way to the upstairs bathtub.

"I will clean this mess up when he is out of the bath," I said. I turned my back and when I turned around, I saw her standing in front of the highchair tray eating the pawed remains of Noah's meal.

Fury swept over me. How I loathed maternal coercion.

"It's garbage," I said angrily. I planted Noah on the kitchen floor. I lifted the tray off its base and carried it to the garbage pail. I stepped on the pedal, the garbage can lid swung open, and I dumped the remains of Noah's meal into the garbage. "You don't have to eat garbage," I said, my heart full of rage.

Hearing my angry tone of voice, Noah started to cry.

"Terrible, terrible to waste," Oma said with dignity. She stooped to the floor to pick up a bit of rye bread wet with saliva.

"It is nutrition," she said. "Nutrition . . ."

I bent down and scooped Noah into my arms. He leaned his cheek on my shoulder, smearing bright orange sweet potato on my white shirt.

"Damn it," I said as I swept out of the kitchen. This is my house. My baby. How dare she reproach me?

Of course, she had not reproached me.

I had reproached her.

Given her past, how could she not be put off by my wild-child style of feeding her grandson? She who had survived not one, but two, world wars.

I hated her.

But I hated myself more.

(It turns out, nothing is simple. When I told this story to John, how surprised I was when he took *my* side. That's when John told me about the painful pus-filled boils that erupted on his backside and legs when he was very small—he couldn't tolerate the cream that Oma forced him to drink to fatten him up. When cream disappeared from the shops in Lielvārde during the war, so did John's skin condition.)

43. Gourmet Food for Babies

I wasn't interested in everyday fare. Like a lot of eighties home cooks, I worshipped at the altar of Rosso and Lukins's *The Silver Palate Cookbook*. In our house, beef tenderloin, crown roast of pork, and medallions of veal were Saturday night "bring the baby" fare. (It helped that John Dewar, a world-class butcher, was located in Newton Centre. Julia Child shopped there.) A heavy oak door separated the kitchen from the dining room in our hundred-year-old Foursquare. Babies notwithstanding, I plated in the kitchen. The plates were heated, which didn't stop the food from getting cold when diapers needed changing.

44. Doing Our Best

Oma continued to bake rye bread. But soon came the calls from her housing complex that her stove, her flat, her entire floor had filled with smoke because she had forgotten to take the bread out of the oven. Her living alone was becoming a problem.

The solution seemed clear to Oma: our new house was plenty big and she should move in with us. (She had, after all, given us a wedding gift of five thousand dollars to help with the down payment.)

When John told her that was not possible, Oma called Ilze, who was now fifteen, and insisted that Ilze pressure her father into changing his mind.

I was shocked by Oma's ruthlessness. John was not.

I reminded Oma of a bit of not-so-ancient history: After John's father died and before moving into her current apartment, Oma had lived with her sons: First with Ivars and his wife, and later with John and Liz. In both cases her arrival heralded the beginning of the end of these marriages. Oma didn't cause these ruptures, but her presence certainly didn't help. I explained to Oma that three children depended on John's and my marriage succeeding and we had to put their needs above everything else. I reminded her that I was a writer. I worked at home and I needed my privacy.

Oma still wanted to live with us.

I told her that was not possible. "I am sorry," I said. "We are doing our best."

"What if that's not good enough?" Oma asked.

45. Force Meets Force

I couldn't stand the way John never threw anything away. Not the mug with the broken handle or the dish with the chipped rim. Not the scratched red enamel skillet, or the broken wooden chair. Not the khakis with frayed cuffs, and not the wooden clogs that hurt his feet. And, most especially, not the glass vase with the slender top and pear-shaped base that he kept on a shelf above the scratched metal desk he'd bought for five dollars in Central Square. He kept the vase, he said, because it reminded him of his ex-wife's round bottom.

Regarding all broken objects he said: *"Ça peut encore servir."*

Regarding our unlovely furnishings he said, "I don't see the problem."

Regarding the glass vase, he said, "It's mine. I like it."

Each of these pronouncements had the ring of papal infallibility. In spheres other than domestic John loathed bullying, but regarding our home, a different person surfaced.

I was confused.

It made no sense to me that a man who could ponder the correct design of wine glasses from September to November; a man whose perfectionistic indecision ruled out shopping together, leaving me no choice three days before Thanksgiving but to buy two dozen wine glasses on sale at Bloomingdales; a man whose concern with design caused him to respond to my last-minute purchase with a connoisseur's disdain. How could a man with standards so high be so oblivious to my aesthetic concerns? True, the factory-made Czechoslovakian glasses were ersatz cut glass, but I thought they would do until we could afford better. I thought they spoke to the dark woodwork and built-in china cabinets in our dining room. But no! Had I no taste? Had I dressed myself in hot pink and turquoise plaid with matching pink plastic handbag and shoes, my mate's judgment could not have been more scathing. Did I not care for the integrity of modern design? Did I not understand that form must follow function? My head swam. I simply could not comprehend how a man who disdained faux cut glass could disregard the disorder that bloomed around him like algae in a warm pond.

John responded to my complaints about our house—its clutter, its hand-me-down everything, its lack of style—with the suggestion that I transform myself into his ex-wife. Hadn't she done a bang-up job in the kitchen of his old house decorating with yellow contact paper! Where was my imagination? My thrifty ability to pull rabbits out of hats? No matter that the two of us were different women: when domesticity was the subject, his first wife was a paragon of virtue, and I, a Philip Rothian shrew. (Note the lurking Jewish reference.)

We'd been married for two years. We lived in a pricey town. We had a house with an 18 percent mortgage, a baby, two daughters to help support, childcare expenses, two cars, no liquid savings, and a shared taste for high quality food. We had little money to spend fixing up a house. That was a fact. But the fight wasn't about facts.

In early May, in the midst of a soul-murdering late spring snowstorm, John flew to sunny Los Angeles to spend a week at the Malibu campus of Hughes Research Laboratory. There, in short sleeves, he would talk science with the founder of the field in which he (John) would soon make his mark. Lunch would be eaten out of doors. I was so discombobulated by jealousy that, after dropping Noah off at his babysitter's, I heedlessly crossed two lanes of traffic to make an illegal U turn. Horns honked as drivers slammed on their brakes. The big-bellied Newton cop who'd seen my perilous maneuver motioned me over to the side of Washington Street. He stuck his head into my car window, shook his head at me, wrote me a ticket and said, "Lady, I don't know what your problem is, but you better wake up."

I could have killed someone.

I could have killed myself.

I could have killed somebody's child.

I could have killed my child!

I went home and, instead of sitting down at my desk to write about Dr. William Morton's 1846 discovery of the anesthetic properties of ether (I had a gig writing for Massachusetts General Hospital), I went on a domestic rampage.

I started in the basement. I schlepped a cracked bicycle helmet, every broken dish and cup waiting to be repaired, and cartons of musty paperbacks outside, dumping them in the garbage. Into the back of the station wagon I hoisted a moth-eaten rug, enough moldy camping gear to fell six Boy Scouts with asthma, a fondue pot we had received as a wedding gift, a toaster oven that didn't work, plus other miscellaneous housewares. These were destined for Goodwill. Then I attacked the upstairs closets. I was on a roll now. I had lost weight since Noah was born. I threw out ten years of my own clothing—ripped it all out of the closet, stuffing it all into plastic bags, including the honey-colored wrap-around alpaca coat with the hood that my friend Lara had given me and that I still miss. On

John's side of the closet, I contented myself with throwing away those damned wooden clogs that hurt his feet. I left his office intact except for that fucking vase, which I smashed against the side of a metal garbage can.

And what happened when John returned home from California on Saturday afternoon? At first, nothing happened. Most of what I had dumped was junk—how long does it take a busy man to notice that a chipped white plate decorated with pink flowers is missing? I could have waited a very long time for John to notice that the clogs that he had bought twenty-three years ago in Helsinki were absent. As for the vase, I am not sure how long it would have taken him to notice it was gone. I don't think he looked at it very much. He just liked having it. But silent revenge wasn't my style. I couldn't keep my mouth shut. On Sunday afternoon, with Noah asleep in his crib and us in our bedroom, the blue-and-white Marimekko duvet peeled back as we prepared for a Sunday-afternoon-welcome-home marital tryst, I spoiled the mood by telling John I had thrown out his clogs and his pear-shaped vase.

What was it that George Bush called the beginning of the second Iraqi war? The one he stupidly started? Shock and Awe. That was John's response to my acts of aggression.

His face got white. A mask fell over his features. His body tensed and his hands curled into fists.

His steely eyes stared at me with contempt.

"How dare you," he asked, his voice low, "how dare you destroy my things?"

My voice wasn't low. "How dare I?" I shouted. "How dare

you bury me alive in junk? How dare you keep that 'souvenir of wives past' in my house? My house!"

"You may never touch my things. Never," John said. "You have never known want, and you have no idea of the value of anything."

"The value of a glass bottle that reminds you of your ex-wife's ass?"

"The clogs I bought in Helsinki. Oma's plates that I intended to repair. These things have meaning. You have no respect. Not everything can be replaced, you know. The world is a dark place. War can come again. Someday we may need these things you have thrown away."

"Oh, spare me your eschatological rants."

"You are a spoiled and useless good-for-nothing. A lazy, useless wench."

What an archaic term, what a peculiar choice of words, I thought as I raised my hand and slapped him across the face. Not hard. But hard enough.

The room got still. Time stopped.

John looked at me. "You may not do that," he said, lifting his hand and slapping me across my face precisely as I had slapped him. Not hard. But hard enough.

I was stunned. Silent.

"Oh," I said, and stepped away.

In a split second something was settled between us. Force had met force and there had been a standoff. John was stronger physically than I, much stronger, but I was more volatile. I knew from now on that no matter how furious I was at John,

I would not raise my hand to him. Because he wouldn't let me. I respected him for that. I loved him for that. Nothing else was resolved that day. Sometimes I think nothing else has ever been resolved between us. But at that moment, standing face to face, the sun shining in our bedroom window, the patterned sky-blue-and-white duvet drawn back inviting us to bed, our child peacefully sleeping in his crib in his room at the other end of the hallway, it was enough. What existed between us was enough.

46. Page Road

We lived on a street, only one block long, called Page Road. Eighteen houses—Victorians and Foursquares built around 1900. There were some old-timers living on the street, but most of our neighbors were couples in their thirties (John was older, forty-four when Noah was born) with two careers who had started their families a little later than the norm. Nobody was rich—this wasn't the fancy part of Newton—but no one was poor, either. The yards were small. The kids, when they were big enough, played together. This swing set, that tree house, more or less common property. The parents, the kids, we cooked out, we hung out, we did Halloween. We shared childcare. This world was so circumscribed, so safe, that when Noah was three, we let him walk by himself to a nearby neighbor's house to play after supper.

Turned out I was not a dark-woodwork, period-architecture kind of a person—I did not love our house. (In truth, I loathed it.) But I loved Page Road. It was Camelot.

47. Our Claim to Fame

We were the neighborhood foodies.

Brunches, lunches, dinners. Platters of pesto chicken. Platters of grilled flank steak. Platters of corn pudding. Blueberry pies in the summer. Apple pies in the fall. I invited everyone. Ilze and Sarma and their teenage friends. The twenty-somethings who rented our third-floor apartment, whom we incorporated into our family. Friends and neighbors and colleagues in their thirties and forties. Family members who were older than that. Our guests came from every decade. I was proud of that.

Sometimes I would lie in bed trying to figure how many people dined at our house in a single year. Two hundred? Three hundred? More?

God only knows how much money we spent.

But it worked. We built a life centered around the table that accommodated our melded family and our oddball selves. Not only that: we enjoyed ourselves.

48. Words to Live By

Our family motto: Three Celebrations a Day.

49. Testament

My cooking evolved as cooking does—but the notion of food as celebration never faltered. We honored what we consumed. We commented on the quality of every apple from the orchard and every honeydew melon that John doused with a squirt of lime juice after slicing it carefully with a recently sharpened knife—keeping the knives sharp was one of John's things. We commented on the crackle of the crust of each loaf of bread. The deep rich brown of the sear. The earthy, oniony, elegance of a well-poached leek. The seasons changed. The tastes and fragrances changed. We changed. But always, we honored the food. And in so doing we honored each other.

50. Bilingual

During the first three years of Noah's life, John spoke Latvian to him and English to me, and I spoke English to John and Noah. My stepdaughters spoke Latvian to their father and English to me, and English or Latvian to Noah, depending on the circumstance; and Noah spoke English early and often to me and his sisters, and he spoke a few Latvian words to his father.

I did not find this arrangement congenial. I hated having my family divided by language. I hated not knowing what John was saying to the girls and to Noah. I hated feeling excluded. At birthday and holiday dinners attended by various members of the Melngailis clan, I would exit the kitchen triumphantly carrying a capon stuffed with wild rice or a veal shoulder roast prepared à la Marcella Hazan only to have the flow of conversation abruptly halt when I arrived at the dining room table. An awkward silence would follow while my husband and in-laws decided if they were going to switch to English or, linguistically speaking, ignore my presence. How could it be that at my own table in my own home with my own husband and family, my own language—the language that defined my identity— could be treated like a bad smell emanating from my body. I responded to this rejection with my usual stubborn refusal. I would not renounce what was mine. I would not allow myself to be undermined and erased. I paid lip service to being a bilingual family, but my words were not sincere.

Noah detected my falsehood. When he was three and a half, he stared into his father's blue eyes and loudly said, "SPEAK ENGLISH!" John did something I would never have predicted: he capitulated. From then on, our family shared a common language. At bedtime, when I read *Mother Goose* and *Winnie-the-Pooh* and Beatrix Potter and fairytales and folktales from every corner of the globe, John lay at end of the bed absorbing a world of stories previously unknown to him.

Finally, we were united under the umbrella of one language. When the five of us were together we spoke English, though John continued to speak Latvian to the girls, and he continued to drive them to Latvian school on Saturdays and Latvian camp in the summer. When Noah was old enough, he went to Jewish Sunday school (reform, of course). He attended day camp in our neighborhood. Later, when he was older, he went to a sleepaway camp, neither Latvian nor Jewish, in New Hampshire. So long as we lived in Newton, John attended the monthly meeting of his folklore group, but with the exception of Midsummer Day, the two of us rarely socialized with members of the Latvian community. For a long time, I thought I had orchestrated this split—but perhaps not, because John later told me that when he tried to hire a Latvian-speaking babysitter for Noah, one tart-tongued granny told him that if Latvian was so important, he shouldn't have married me. Then she hung up the phone.

By strategy or by default, over time my language, my social expectations, and my religion shaped our family life. This was not something we discussed, but John seemed okay with the way we were living. His career had taken off and he was busier than he had ever been. He left home early and rarely returned before 7:30 p.m. Twice a week when he visited Oma, (first in assisted living, later in the nursing home associated with this facility) he got home even later. Moreover, he often traveled for work. John's allegiance to Latvian causes, his sense of himself as fundamentally Latvian, did not change. He continued to call himself a pagan, although I did convince him that we both needed to attend his niece's confirmation at the Latvian Lutheran Church. But in a functional sense these things moved to the back burner. Work and family, and our friends from John's work and my work, and from our neighborhood, ate up most of our available time.

I thought I had won our ethnic war.

51. Christmas

It was okay to have a Christmas tree, John said, because Christmas trees were pagan not Christian. And it was okay to celebrate Christmas because, well, we had the tree, right? Before the divorce, John's family celebrated Christmas on Christmas Eve, as is the Latvian tradition. After the divorce, dividing the holiday in two was easy. The girls spent Christmas Eve with their dad and me and Noah, and Christmas day with their mother and stepfather and his children. In Germany on our honeymoon, I had bought several dozen nonreligious Christmas tree ornaments—shiny red apples made of balsa wood, small white birds decorated with real feathers, miniature wooden toys and bears. Year after year I got a kick out of adding to this collection.

As to how we celebrated? The year I was pregnant we spent Christmas Eve with John's brother and sister-in-law at the large house they still owned jointly, though they no longer lived together. (Ivars was living with the woman who became his second wife.) Oma was present, as was John's Uncle Edwards, plus three generations of in-laws from Ivar's wife's side. The holiday was straight out of E. T. A. Hoffmann. Swags of fresh greenery adorning every surface. Mistletoe. Real candles in little silver holders burning on the tree. Ilze and Sarma and their girl cousins, dressed in taffeta party dresses, were required to perform—Ilze played the piano—or sing or recite a poem. For dinner, John's nephew Nils, a recent college grad, slow-roasted a goose and used the excess goose fat to braise cabbage for hours and hours until it resembled silken amber—sauerkraut for the gods. I ate and ate, my hearty appetite applauded by all—regarding pregnant eating, the rules are turned upside down. A woman's hearty appetite earns praise. The following year, when Noah was five months old, I invited the girls and two other couples with babies—both of whom happened to be Jewish—for Christmas Eve dinner at our house. I made a standing rib roast with roasted potatoes. No sauerkraut to be found. I don't know if it was the break with tradition, the absence of her cousins, or my Jewish misapprehension, but halfway through the meal Sarma fell asleep, her face resting on the table.

I had to do better. (Why I believed this problem was mine alone to solve, well, that was another issue.)

I stumbled around for a few years. I spent a lot of money and still bought the wrong gifts. Guess what? Teenage girls really do not want you to buy clothes for them. But after a while we found our way to our own traditions.

On Christmas Eve the five of us would eat a ceremonial dinner (beef tenderloin, potatoes gratin, and French-cut string beans). Before dessert we would move from the dining room table to the living room where our pagan Christmas tree was covered with nonreligious ornaments and the tiny white lights the girls favored. (At their mom's house, Ilze and Sarma had to tolerate the multicolored lights that were preferred by their step-siblings.) John would build a fire and I would retrieve the Belgian chocolates from their hiding place. These were the richest, most luxurious chocolates for sale in Boston. (After Neuhaus, we discovered Burdick.) John would cut each truffle and bonbon, each caramel and nougat, into five little pieces, so all could taste all, and then we would open our presents very slowly, one at a time, savoring each Benetton sweater, dangle of silver, and white porcelain platter from Crate&Barrel—every year, at the suggestion of their mother, the girls gave us a white serving piece, until eventually I had a collection—as buttery chocolate slowly melted in our mouths. (In the interest of full disclosure: Noah was exempted from the "open slowly" rule and, moreover, he preferred M&M's to truffles.)

52. Hometown Girl

Boston wasn't endless like New York, but it was prettier and more manageable for a working mom with a car. Moreover, fifty minutes north and east of our house were some of the most gorgeous and (relatively speaking) undiscovered beaches in the world. True, this was the North Shore (not Cape Cod), and, yes, the water at Crane Beach was cold enough to deaden bodily sensation, still the endless sweep of sand and sea made me wildly happy. In July and August, we'd drive to the beach in the midafternoon when the parking lot was starting to empty, remain on the beach as the light turned pink, then shower in the bathhouse and make our way to Woodman's of Essex, where fried clam had been invented a hundred years earlier and the lobsters were steamed just hours after they were caught.

53. Landing

Professionally, too, I felt at home.

I continued to write freelance articles for magazines and newspapers—a profile I did for *Ms.* magazine led to me writing a second book. In addition, I developed a sideline, producing publications for teaching hospitals and universities, which Boston possessed in abundance. I learned a ton doing this work, and wherever I went I got to be part of a team, which I liked, because freelance journalism is lonely.

54. A Sweet Ending

As her memory faded, Oma was no longer able to care for herself. In her last two years, Oma lived in an assisted living facility located ten minutes from the MIT campus, where John visited her several times a week. Often, he'd find her drawing pictures depicting the farm where she had lived as a child. The last time he saw her, Oma asked John where he had tied up his horse, then she grabbed his arm, squeezed it hard, and looked intensely in his eyes. She died in her sleep that night. She was ninety-one.

55. Yellow Wagon

John heard about a Latvian guy from Hartford, Connecticut, who had installed a bread oven in his parents' basement and was baking a tasty version of *rupjmaize*. Yes, I believe it contained wheat, but it tasted good. Ten loaves cost as much to ship from Hartford as two.

John took orders in our neighborhood, and when the rye bread arrived, we would keep three loaves—two for us and one for Liz, who would reciprocate with apples from the orchard she and her second husband owned. John would pile the rest on Noah's bright yellow Fisher-Price wagon, the one with wide wheels that we took to the beach, and the two of them would make their way up and down the small streets of our neighborhood.

Not always the schmooziest guy, John had a talent for selling rye bread. He built a market by wooing our neighbors, children and adults, with his line of patter and plentiful free samples. When he found a truly receptive child, John sealed the deal with games of chess played in front of our fireplace, followed by a snack of rye bread, sardines, and hot chocolate. This, John remembers, was the very treat relief workers from the United Nations fed "the starving children of Europe" after the war. It's a testament to John's power of persuasion that Noah, who saw himself as a regular American kid, and so many of his friends happily consumed these foods from a far-away time and place.

The Hartford rye bread became our culinary signature. In the winter we sat in front of the fireplace with our friends drinking wine and eating rye bread topped with melted Jarlsberg cheese and Dijon mustard—whatever its shortcomings as a cheese, Jarlsberg melts gooey and is perfect for an open-faced sandwich. Thor of the North, i.e. John, did not believe in sandwiches with covers. In the summer, we drank beer and ate hunks of grilled sausage on top of rye bread. With sauerkraut.

56. Orthodontia

In John's view there were virtually no health problems that rye bread could not cure. The prevalence of crooked teeth—and expensive orthodontia—among the children of the American middle class? John was convinced crooked teeth resulted from eating soft white bread. The cure? Foods such as Latvian rye bread that resisted when you bit into them.

Of course, I scoffed.

But John's intuition was correct.

Turns out bone growth in the jaw and elsewhere can be enhanced by mechanical stress. Gnawing on hard foods in childhood stimulates the "piezoelectric effect," a complicated biological process that mobilizes bone-building cells. In other words, forceful chewing when young promotes jawbone formation and tooth alignment. As the man said: Eat rye bread and put the orthodontist out of business.

57. Chewing

Chewing turned out to be a bigger deal than I understood. Those soft foods that required virtually no chewing did more than deprive bone of needed stimulation. As the food writer Maria Speck explained in an essay called "A Gift of Grains," foods without substance stripped eating of purpose and pleasure. "Chewing [is] heavenly, especially when it involves the crackle of a crusty dark bread or the crunch of whole grain cracker," Speck wrote. Then she offered an insight that over time changed my life. By forcing her to focus on what she was eating, Speck wrote, chewing "slows me down," and in so doing it "civilizes me."

Chewing on a piece of dense, grainy bread civilized her.

In time, I would come to believe that chewing on a slice of Latvian rye bread slathered with peanut butter, or smashed avocado, or any number of other delicious foods civilized me, too, teaching me to slow down and attend to what I was eating and, in so doing, teaching me to recognize when I was full.

All this sounds as if it should have been obvious. But for me, it was not.

Hanging out in front of our fireplace with our friends Diana and Richard, eating what Diana always called "John's bread,"

I was starting to understand the meaning of rye bread; but I wasn't there yet.

58. Bigot 1

One Sunday morning our weekend pillow talk wandered into ethnically explosive territory. Such as, the complicity of some Latvians in the murder of 70,000 Latvian Jews during World War II. I was shocked when John, by way of explaining, suggested some sort of historical tit-for-tat had been at work. "Because," he told me earnestly, "the leaders of the Latvian communist party—the guys who sold out Latvia's republic— they were all Jewish." (In fact, some were, and some were not.)

"Are you saying the seventy thousand Latvian Jews who were murdered were communists and therefore deserved to die?" I asked. "What about the ones who were greedy capitalists?"

John didn't rise to the bait, reiterating instead that Jewish communists had sold out the Latvian republic.

"You advocate the punishment of seventy thousand for the crimes of a few?" I asked.

"I'm not advocating anything. But people have their reasons . . ."

This disturbing conversation drove me from our bed. I went to the bathroom to escape. I looked at myself in the mirror. What a mess I was. Winter pale. My hair, disheveled and needing a haircut. It occurred to me that I was married to a bigot. I found this thought oddly comforting. The problem in our marriage wasn't me. It was him.

59. Bigot 2

After I had gotten my fill of hating John, I thought about my own xenophobia. I didn't talk about being Jewish as often as John talked about being Latvian, but that didn't mean being Jewish wasn't the lens through which I gazed at the world.

I recalled a phone conversation with my grandmother that had taken place some time before. I'd been bragging about Noah, how smart he was. I told my grandmother that I had been making dinner when I realized Noah wasn't in the kitchen with me. I went looking and found him lying peacefully on the carpet in the family room.

"What are you doing?" I had asked him.

"I am thinking about numbers," he answered. He was three and a half.

"*Lang lebn zayn eydish kop,*" my grandmother had responded in the Yiddish of her birthplace, Belarus.

"Long live his Yiddish head," I had repeated, happily taking credit for our son's obvious genius, though his Latvian father had a PhD in theoretical physics and the only time I thought about numbers was when trying to figure out how much to tip.

Did I, like John, see the world through an ethnic lens? Was ethnicity my default frame of reference?

And did I, like John, think my group was superior?

I wasn't sure that I did, but I wasn't sure that I did not.

60. No Longer Newlyweds

When you have been married for a while, you learn that your mate has blind spots and prejudices and perhaps you do, too.

You learn that libido ebbs and flows and sex, sometimes thrilling, can also be boring. You learn that most arguments are
circular, and that money really does matter. You learn the
old-fashioned virtues—forbearance especially—are important
and that laughter and a shared sense of irony are as important
as mutual attraction.

61. The Peanut Butter Joke
John liked jokes.

The peanut butter joke was his favorite:

On Monday at lunchtime, Al sits down with his friends,
opens his lunch bag, peeks inside, and throws the bag across
the room. "Yuck!" he says in disgust. "Peanut butter."

On Tuesday Al opens his lunch bag and looks inside. "Christ
Almighty," he shouts. "Peanut butter." Again, he throws the
bag across the room.

On Wednesday, after Al has once again thrown the hated
peanut butter sandwich across the room, a coworker inter-
venes: "Al," he says, "if you hate peanut butter so much, why
don't you ask your wife to make you something else?"

"Oh, no," Al says. "No. I pack my own lunch."

62. The Man in the Mirror
The fact that John thought the peanut butter joke was funny
went a long way with me. Although he did not always show it,
John possessed emotional intelligence and he knew we humans
are often our own worst enemies.

I loved him for knowing that.

63. Susan Tells Me

It was a snappy afternoon in early March. My friend Susan and I had just barreled up the long, steep incline leading to the top of West Newton Hill. Our hearts were beating fast and our cheeks were rosy, but now came the fun part, walking and talking and catching up as we traversed one of the prettiest neighborhoods in Newton. Only on this particular day it was I who did most of the talking.

I was riled up that afternoon. John was in a loopy manic phase. He wasn't sleeping and consequently I wasn't sleeping, which was undermining my clarity of mind, although I was supposed to be the sane one.

Mostly I didn't talk about John's bipolar disorder.

Mostly I didn't think about it. Unless John's mood was going off the rails, and then it was hard to think about anything else.

A psychotherapist licensed to prescribe psych meds, Susan treated patients like John and she knew a lot about bipolar disease. She also "got" John's eccentricities and she cared about him. Which made sense, because he really liked her and went out of his way to let her know that.

"It happens every year in February as the days get longer," I panted. "He starts waking up earlier and earlier, full of energy. There's a cycle that builds . . . at first, I enjoy how communicative he is, but then he can't contain himself. . . . Eventually he crashes."

"Does he go on shopping sprees?' Susan asked.

"He doesn't spend a lot of money, but he buys weird stuff.

Once he bought three dozen wooden hangers at the Beth Israel thrift store!"

"Drinking?" Susan asked.

"Not more than a beer or two. But he is full of emotion. He needs me to listen to him. It doesn't matter what else I am doing. He tears up telling me that he loves me. Part of me likes it, that he is so wide open, but then I feel assailed by his intensity."

"Violent?" Susan asked.

"Tae kwon do helps him keep the lid on, but I feel as if I am walking on eggshells. Like he could blow. It seems so sad that he can't put the two sides of himself together. Most of the time he's so buttoned up, and then, when he's manic, he's wide open and . . . and he just can't seem to modulate." I stop walking and look at Susan. "I told you that he had a major breakdown when he was twenty-eight, right?"

Susan nodded. "You know," she said, "there's a lot of new research establishing a correlation between bipolar disorder and childhood trauma, war, and displacement."

"Childhood trauma," I repeated. "Well, he certainly experienced that."

PART TWO

A Displaced Person

1. The Imprint of the Past

In his family memoir, *The Girl from Human Street*, Roger Cohen, a *New York Times* columnist based in London, wrote about the multigenerational impact of childhood trauma, war, and dislocation on his mother June. Cohen blamed his mother's severe mental illness—she suffered from bipolar disorder and twice attempted suicide—on her genetic inheritance, of course, but also on the impact of history on her psyche. This he referred to as "the imprint of the past."

"New opportunity is only one side of the immigrant story, its bright star," Cohen wrote. "The other side, its black sun, is displacement and loss. In each generation on the move, members of my family have been unable to come to terms with the immense struggle involved in burying the past, losing an identity, and embracing a new life—as if the bipolarity from which several suffered were just that, a double existence attempting to bridge the unbridgeable . . ."

2. Racing Across Europe in a Car

At least once a year John traveled to Europe for his work. Sometimes I tagged along. On this occasion, Noah and I joined him. Traveling solo or en famille, John would rent a car and drive from one European destination to another, stopping to visit people and places to which he was attached. Distance was no issue: he liked driving. Racing across Europe in a car, I called his mode of travel.

3. Noah in Egg (January 1993)

The three of us were in Germany. Noah was nine years old. He was on winter break, as was John. We had been in Heidelberg visiting Manfred (a German scientist with whom John collaborated), his wife, Ursula, and their four irrepressible daughters. Now we were staying in Stuttgart with John's architect friends Gert and Gerta, the ones who'd hosted us on our honeymoon. This morning, with John at the wheel, the five of us were piled into our rental heading south to Lake Constance. On the way, we stopped to tour Birnau Abbey, a soaring baroque church bedecked in white porcelain and gold that simultaneously enthralled and appalled me. Later, in Friedrichshafen, a small city on Lake Constance, Gert and Gerta led us on a tour of the recently opened concert hall that they had designed.

And then, as the sun sank, we arrived in Egg. John's Brigadoon, where he lived when he was Noah's age. It was 4 p.m. We were tired. I had not known Egg was on our itinerary.

"Why are we here?" I asked.

John insisted that we get out of the car. He took Gerta's arm. As the five of us slowly traversed the dirt road running past the village's weary stucco houses and its leafless trees, John leaned toward his friends to make a point. The three of them spoke in German, excluding Noah and me. As we approached each structure, John peered expectantly into the yard, searching for signs of life. There were none. Even the racehorses were gone. We had arrived at ultima Thule.

Noah was silent, apparently disinterested. I was silent, too. Ten years of marriage and, still, I was unable to fathom the hunger for roots that compelled John to return to this depopulated German village where no one awaited his return.

On that winter afternoon I was not unkind, not overtly so. I was just a person thinking her own thoughts, staging her own perpetual rebellion, reacting to her own endangered sense of agency. A person who would rather be somewhere else.

I did not know why John chose to walk arm and arm with Gert and Gerta through the village while ignoring his son and me. I was not curious why this might be. Being in Egg felt like a choice John inflicted on us. On that chilly January day, I did not excavate John's motivations in order to explain father to son and son to father.

YEARS LATER, WHEN working on this book, I asked Noah what he remembered from our visit to Egg when he was nine.

"I didn't get it," Noah told me. "My father was a big deal scientist. Everyone knew those were the smartest guys in the world. When his students came to our house, I could see they looked up to him. I looked up to him, too. We played chess. He was the soccer coach. He was different than other dads. He'd been born in Europe. He spoke languages and talked a lot about rye bread. I got that. But Europe had nothing to do with that shit-kicking dirt road and those pathetic houses. I didn't understand what that weird place had to do with him or with me. I didn't know why he had dragged me there." Looking back, I regret my misapprehension. Had I understood what drove John to revisit Egg that afternoon—his perpetual need to reknit his fractured self, and his desire to show his son the village where he lived during formative years of his childhood—I might have been more helpful, more generous. Instead, John was wordless with Noah and me. As was so often the case in relation to what he cared about the most, he could not, or would not, share his thoughts or his feelings with us.

4. Definition of an Exile

A person who lives among those who do not share his story or may not care about his story. Someone whose ideas about history, art, religion, nature, birth, and death are deemed foreign or weird or incomprehensible. Often his wife and children are among those who do not comprehend.

5. Primal Journey 1

After many road trips racing across Europe in a car with John, stopping to revisit places from his past that he had visited many times before, I began to understand this mode of travel was not a choice for John. It was a psychological imperative.

6. Primal Journey 2

Skip this section if you have an aversion to psychological explanations.

I believe that John's habit of racing across Europe in a car is not really voluntary. I think traveling like this is rooted in his past when he and his family twice fled from east to west to avoid onrushing catastrophe. Traveling by ship and by rail in 1944 and again by rail in 1945, five-year-old John saw things, felt things, no child should see or feel. And yet, by moving, moving, moving, his parents kept their family safe. I think of these wartime voyages as John's primal journeys—shocking and formative in a way that resembles Freud's primal scene, in which Freud believed a child accidentally glimpsed his parents' sexual embrace. Many of the judgments of the good Doctor Freud (or bad Doctor Freud, depending on your point of view) turned out to be incorrect. But his understanding that some sights once seen, some experiences once lived, carve crevasses inside a person's very soul, unconsciously shaping how he later lives his life, is, I think, impossible to contest. From the cauldron that was his childhood, John's restless need to move was reinforced, as was his insistence that he be in control of the mode of travel and his abiding nostalgia for where he has been, and where he is no more. Remembering, for John, is not enough. He must travel there. He must race across Europe in a car, visiting the places where he has lived, in search of some wholeness forever beyond his grasp.

7. The Hegira (Riga, 1944)

John and his family were not the only Latvians fleeing for their lives, sprinting westward across Europe in the last months of World War II, seeking to escape an enemy whose villainy they believed exceeded Hitler's. Millions of Eastern Europeans did as they did, running toward the safety of what one Latvian woman described as "the mythical west."

Many of those who fled—including John's parents, Jakobīne and Jānis—knew from experience what it meant to save your skin by escaping. They knew this because they had been refugees once before. During World War I, when he was in his mid-twenties and she in her late teens, to avoid the carnage taking place on Latvian soil, hundreds of thousands of Latvians fled eastward into Russia. This first displacement prepared them for the hardships they were to face in 1944, when they fled in the opposite direction. To be twice exiled in the twentieth century. This was the peculiar fate of Latvians and millions of others residing in the lowland countries between Germany and Russia that historian Timothy Snyder famously named the Bloodlands.

Bloodlands, indeed. On the crowded European continent and here on our side of the Atlantic, geography, it turned out, was destiny.

8. Geography Is Destiny 1

I have friends and family born in Latvia, Germany, Nigeria. El Salvador. Turkey. Brittany. Japan. They understand the impact of place on destiny. They are familiar with the suffering inflicted on individuals and nations by invading armies, colonialism, civil war, and defeat. While we, by which I mean a subset of comfortable white, native-born Americans, we of the vast and impregnable fortress, we imagine ourselves exempt. This, despite the weight and horror of our own ambiguous actions here in our birthland and abroad. Born yesterday, we are as sunny as babes. The rest of the world marvels at our blindness.

9. The Rehearsal: World War I

John's father, Jānis, was a twenty-four-year-old student studying agronomy (the science of agriculture) in Riga in 1914 when World War I broke out. Jānis Melngailis would have been drafted by Czar Nicholas II and sent to the front to fight the Germans, had he not been lucky: the Czar exempted only children from the draft and Jānis had no siblings. Instead of serving in the military, Jānis spent the war years in Moscow, where his university was relocated. Not that living in Moscow was a picnic. By the end of the war, the per-person bread ration was reduced to half a kilo per week—slightly more than a pound. Living conditions were better in the countryside near the forests, where Jānis worked in jobs that amounted to paid internships—in his day they were called "practicums." Sometime before the Czar and his family were murdered in July of 1918, Jānis returned to Latvia with his degree. His homecoming coincided with the war of independence that led to Latvia declaring itself a republic. Again, his status as an only child exempted him from fighting.

John's mother, Jakobīne Zile, was an eighteen-year-old aspiring pharmacist when war was declared in 1914. Her family's modest farm, forty miles northeast of Riga, was located uncomfortably near the German–Russian front. Skirmishes were common. Returning one night from the local tavern, Jakobīne's father was killed under mysterious circumstances. His unmarked body was discovered in the road, the apparent victim of mustard gas. Following his death, Jakobīne, her mother, her two sisters, and two brothers boarded a train heading south and east to Kislovodsk, in the northern Caucasus region of Russia. There, 1550 miles from home, Jakobīne's interest in medicine and knowledge of healing compounds paid off. Though refugees had a hard time finding work, Jakobīne landed a job working at a pharmacy. From 1915 to 1918, she was her family's sole support. (At least that was how she remembered it.) When the Ziles returned home to Latvia, they found squatters living on their farm. Taking pity, they allowed the squatters to remain, unaware that these strangers were infected with tuberculosis. Jakobīne's mother contracted TB— Jakobīne nursed her mother through what turned out to be her fatal illness.

Somewhere along the line Jakobīne studied to be a pharmacist and passed her licensing examination. After the death of her mother, she found a job as an apprentice pharmacist in Saulkrasti, a small town near her family's farm. She viewed this position as temporary. Ambitious by nature and a planner, she dreamed of owning her own business. Eventually, with the help of her future husband, she would make this dream a reality.

10. Courtship

Jakobīne met her future husband in 1931, when she was thirty-five years old and living and working in Saulkrasti. For women of her generation, appropriate marriage partners were in short supply—too many young men had died fighting too many wars. An independent thinker, Jakobīne considered having a child without benefit of matrimony. Before taking that drastic step, she let friends and family in Riga know that she was interested in getting married.

Enter John's father. Age forty-one. Handsome. Affable. Never married. An only child with an only child's sunny conviction that his feelings and his needs were of paramount importance. In the daytime Jānis worked as a government land inspector. In the evening, he frequented Riga's cafes and attended the opera wearing a fancy hat and leather gloves. In the 1920s and '30s, Riga was a vibrant place. From the medieval old town to the modern city with its hundreds of eye-popping art nouveau "skyscrapers," its architecture competed with that of much larger capitals, and the arts—especially music, but also painting—thrived there. For a 1924 *National Geographic* magazine, an American writer and photographer visited Riga and wrote that he expected to find a primitive encampment where locals drank reindeer milk. Instead, he found a cosmopolitan city where beautiful women nibbled pastries "light as a summer cloud," the opera was world-class, and "serious dining" began at 11 p.m.

It wasn't until he turned forty (just weeks after the 1929 crash of the American stock market) that Jānis made a serious effort to settle down. A friend told him about a woman living in the countryside, an ambitious pharmacist eager to open her own business, who was looking for a husband.

Jānis took his friend Edwards, a courtly, shell-shocked World War I veteran, with him when he went to meet his future bride. At first Jakobīne did not know what to make of these gentlemen callers from the city. Was one of them interested in her romantically? If so, she preferred Edwards, whose quiet ways and consideration appealed to her. It was Jānis, however, who returned the following week. Soon he proposed.

11. Lielvārde

After marrying (probably in 1932), Jakobīne and Jānis settled in Lielvārde, a town of several thousand on the Daugava River thirty-two miles southeast of Riga, connected to the capital by the railroad. Lielvārde had been flattened during the war and was now busily rebuilding. John's parents acquired land in the center of town near the railroad station where they intended to build a house large enough to accommodate the children they hoped to have and the modern pharmacy Jakobīne intended to operate. The savings Jānis accrued during his long bachelor-hood enabled them to move forward with this ambitious plan. In the meantime, both continued to work and save. According to family lore, Jakobīne first operated her Lielvārde pharmacy in a rundown shop she acquired from the proprietor's widow.

In 1933 Jānis and Jakobīne were granted a permit to build a combined house and pharmacy on their lot near the center of town. One month later, their first child, a son they named Ivars, was born. Their new house came equipped with electric light, wood-fired central heating, plus a modern kitchen and bath. Precisely when they moved in is not clear. The pharmacy was not given a permit to operate until December 1938, by which time Ivars was five. In the interim, she must have run her increasingly successful business out of its old quarters. Genuinely interested in medicine, a proponent, like many Latvians, of naturopathic remedies, and needing very much to be needed, Jakobīne had a great deal to offer. Patients looking for medical advice and treatment flocked to her pharmacy, to the point of angering the local doctor.

12. The Marriage

Theirs was not a conventional love match. Jakobīne and Jānis were loyal to one another throughout their forty years of marriage, and they were compatible, in the sense that they possessed complementary skill sets, and both were profoundly committed to their sons. But for Jakobīne, something—some emotional connection—was missing. What others found charming in Jānis, she disparaged. She objected to his easy charm and his Panglossian expectation that everything would turn out all right, and she denigrated his ability to navigate difficult interpersonal terrain—although this talent, in conjunction with her planning and problem solving, proved to be invaluable during the war. Time and again, Jakobīne told her sons that their father was a disappointment to her. Later she told them that another suitor—perhaps the mysterious one whose picture she carried all her life—would have been a better match. As to his qualities as a mate, Jānis Senior was warm, but not particularly engaged. For companionship, he turned to his loyal friend Edwards, rather than his hard-working, hard-to-please wife. He never questioned his privileged position as the head of the household, the one to which others must defer, although Jakobīne earned twice what he did.

Still Jakobīne took pride in Jānis's good looks and his university degree, and she recognized his intelligence and his fundamental decency: steady by nature, Jānis did not drink to excess and he held a secure job. Like his wife-to-be, he hewed to the center politically.

Human nature being what it is, Jakobīne's assessment of her husband's character did not prevent her from yearning for his approval. (Perhaps her hunger for his approval was the cause, or a cause, of her dissatisfaction.) To please Jānis, she fixed her hair and tried to look stylish. John remembers her squeezing her broad feet into ill-fitting high heels, while simultaneously making fun of women who "put on airs." That Jānis rarely invited her to attend the opera in Riga with him wounded her deeply.

After their marriage, Jānis continued to live and work in the capital during the week. On Friday evenings he traveled by train to Lielvārde. There he spent the weekends luxuriating in the comforts of home with his wife, his child, and his mother, who fought Jakobīne tooth and nail for control of the household. (Jānis refused to take sides, leaving his wife to fight this battle alone.)

Three languages were spoken in the Melngailis household. Latvian, the beloved mother tongue, long banned from official discourse by Russian imperial authorities. German, the language of land barons, capitalists, and high culture. And Russian, the long-entrenched language of the civil bureaucracy and schools. Street signs in Riga were written in all three languages. This multilingual stew reflected Latvia's historic double subjugation—for centuries the Czars controlled Latvia politically while the Germans owned the land.

After suffering a series of miscarriages, Jakobīne, at age forty-three, gave birth to a second baby in February 1939, whom they named Jānis—"John" in English—after his father. Jakobīne and one of her brothers-in-law had recently built a small apartment building on a trolley line in Riga. Jānis, working in Riga, oversaw construction of the building and helped to manage it. The family's future seemed bright.

13. The Second Son

He was a desperately wanted baby born at a perilous moment. His mother and father and his nanny, Mrs. Abel, doted on him. Mrs. Abel spoke German to him and "Little Jāni" grew up bilingual. At six months he lay naked on his stomach on a white bear skin rug gazing solemnly into the camera. He didn't smile—not the style back then, smiling in portraits—but his pale blond hair shone bright, his alabaster skin gleamed, and his aliveness jumped from the page.

Remembering the privations of the last war and haunted by the memory of all those miscarriages, his mother, overly solicitous by nature, worried about her newborn. His body type was long and lean, different from his solidly built brother. His mother feared he was too skinny to withstand hard times. To fatten him up, she forced him to drink the cream that he would forever recall with disgust. He preferred, of course, the *rupjmaize* on which he teethed.

He was overindulged and yet lonely. Long after he learned to walk and run—he loved to run—Mrs. Abel insisted on wheeling him in the pram. He cannot remember playing with other children.

The high point of his week came on Friday in the early evening when Mrs. Abel wheeled him to the train station to greet his father, arriving home for the weekend. He would wait impatiently for the steam-bellowing beast to discharge its passengers. Then, catching a glimpse of his father, he would race to meet him, leaping into his arms.

One Friday, spying his father on the train platform, Little Jāni's timing was off and he leapt too soon and too forcefully.

His father caught him as usual and swung him up in the air, only this time the son's head connected hard and fast with his father's elegant nose.

"Bad boy," his father shouted, opening his arms and willfully dropping his son onto the cement platform, raising his hand to feel his injured nose. Was it broken? Would he be disfigured?

John began to wail, his sobs registering the shock of his hard landing, his injured pride, and something more. A sense of injustice. It wasn't right that he be punished. He hadn't meant to hurt his father.

As Jānis Senior marched off, Mrs. Abel swooped in for the rescue. "There, there," she said, lifting up the disconsolate little boy. "No harm done. No harm at all . . ."

Maybe so, but John never forgot this moment of revelation. His beloved father could be vengeful and unjust.

14. In the Line of Fire

When John was seven months old, Hitler and Stalin signed a treaty dividing up Eastern Europe. Eight days later, Germany invaded Poland. Less than a year after that, the Russians marched into Latvia, staged a communist coup, and deported the president, who died in captivity. (Although the president had been democratically elected, by the time he was deported, he had become an authoritarian with pro-fascist leanings, and he had dissolved political parties in the country.) Other government officials were also deported, imprisoned, or killed. Private property was abolished. Even small businesses like Jakobīne's pharmacy were nationalized. Russian authorities installed one of John's mother's assistants, Miss Rubenstein, a Jewish woman and a communist, to a position in the department overseeing the nationalization of pharmacies. Oma was allowed to continue running her own establishment.

Russian authorities attempted to nationalize small farms, including Jakobīne's family farm, now run by her older brother, Jēkabs, but the farmers fought back. Before the Red Army succeeded in crushing the farmers, Hitler's army, abrogating Germany's treaty with Russia, rolled into Latvia from the west in June of 1941, causing the Russians to flee in the opposite direction. As a parting shot, Stalin ordered the deportation of 15,000 Latvian civilians to Siberia. Most of the male exiles, including Jakobīne's brother, froze to death or died of disease and starvation in Siberian camps far from their families. (Ian Frazier, author of *Travels in Siberia*, opined in a *New Yorker* article that camps in the Siberian gulag were worse than German concentration camps. I find the comparison odious, but it does help to convey the abject horror these exiles—prisoners, really—confronted.) Women and children were often interned in villages and encampments where conditions were only marginally less deadly. After decades of imprisonment, many women and their adult offspring returned home to Latvia, including John's first cousin, Jānis, his growth stunted by starvation.

John's father may have been on the list of those destined for Siberia. The Russian military began mass arrests on Friday, June 13, 1941. Arriving at Riga's Central Railroad station that Friday for his weekly trip to Lielvārde, Jānis Senior learned that the train was not running. Perhaps he saw a flurry of military activity, lines of military vehicles, swarms of heavily armed soldiers. Instinct told him not to return to his Riga apartment and not to wait at the station for train service to Lielvārde to be resumed. Exhibiting the combination of luck, pluck, and smarts that typified how he operated during the war, Jānis Senior decided to walk the fifty kilometers (thirty-two miles) from Riga to Lielvārde.

All over the country that night Russian soldiers seized men in their homes and on the street, escorting them home at gunpoint, ordering them and their family members to quickly pack a few belongings and then ferrying them to Riga's transnational Šķirotava rail station to be transported to the gulag. When Jānis Senior set out on his walk, the sun was still high in the sky. It didn't set until nearly 10 p.m., and it rose again six hours later. Jānis just kept walking. It took him nearly twenty-four hours to arrive in Lielvārde. By then the trains to Siberia had departed and he and his family were safe.

When the German army chased the Russians out in 1941, much of the population greeted them as liberators. Their enthusiasm proved to be ill considered, as the Nazi high command soon began murdering civilians. Jews, of course. As well as communists, socialists, trade unionists, other opponents of German-style fascism, and well, anyone who got in their way.

One of John's first memories speaks to the horror of Nazi mass murder. John remembers hearing his father whispering to his mother about the sound of gunfire and seeing mountains of shoes and other clothing piled high near the tracks as he rode past Rumbula Forest on the train. Rumbula is the site of an infamous December 1941 massacre during which Nazi death squads, with the enthusiastic help of Latvian fascists, in two days shot 25,000 Jews to death, most of them Latvian citizens. At the time of the Rumbula massacre, John was not yet three years old. Perhaps he did overhear his father recounting what he had seen. Or perhaps he remembers his parents discussing this event after the fact. Either way, his parent's sotto voce murmurings about mass murder are among his earliest childhood memories.

Prior to the war, the Jewish community in Latvia had included many groups, not all of whom got along. Religiously, Latvian Jews ran the gamut from extreme religious traditionalism to a forward-looking variety of Judaism that sought to accommodate itself to the modern world. Some modernists, particularly those interested in Zionism, sought to replace Yiddish with Hebrew as the everyday Jewish vernacular. Politically and economically, too, Latvian Jews were a hodgepodge, including among them merchants, manufacturers, doctors and lawyers, artists, opera singers, musicians, peddlers, laborers, union activists, pro-Soviet communists, anarchists, and everything in between. After its founding in 1918, the Latvian Republic had briefly bestowed full political rights on its entire "Hebrew" population. With the rise of German-style fascism in the 1930s, these rights were taken away.

John's parents had no use for Nazi ideology. Jānis Senior might speak ill of the Jewish bankers and Jewish communists he believed were exerting too much influence in his country, but his prejudices were toothless. He certainly didn't wish Jews dead, and he did not approve of Latvia's brutal Arajs militia that employed Gestapo-like tactics. Jakobīne, ever the freethinker, admired Jewish people, identifying with what she saw as their ambition, their commitment to education, their dedication to family, and their outsider status. Before the war all three of her employees at the pharmacy had been Jewish women, a fact that had raised eyebrows among some of her neighbors.

Still, for Jakobīne and Jānis, the Germans who invaded their country in 1941 were unquestionably the lesser of two evils. Like the Russians, the Germans ruled by terror, seizing control of all strategic industries, most especially agriculture, food production, and manufacturing. But the Germans were not opposed to the idea of small business. Somewhere in our attic are official papers, stamped with Nazi insignia, reinstating John's mother's ownership of her pharmacy. John's father spoke fluent Russian and German, which may be why the Nazis put him in charge of a flour mill in Riga, a job requiring him to oversee Russian slave laborers.

Shortly after the German invasion, enlisted men and officers from the German regular army, the Wehrmacht, commandeered the family's house, constructing a communications center in the basement that they manned twenty-four hours a day. The pharmacy continued to operate out of the first-floor storefront. The rest of the first floor belonged to the soldiers and their officers, who bunked in the parlor. The family lived and slept on the second floor. The two groups shared the kitchen and bathroom but did not eat together.

The soldiers treated the family well. They were especially kind to John, who remembers presenting them with his carefully made drawings depicting all the residents of his house—mother,

father, grandmother, older brother, child, soldiers, and officers. John assures me that the enlisted men living in his house
were not Nazis, meaning they were not members of the S.S.
They were Wehrmacht. Regular army. Draftees who told his
parents they thought Hitler was insane. (As to the politics of
their officers, John has no idea, nor does he know what his
parents thought. In retrospect, there is every reason to believe
that as officers these men would have been supporters of the
Nazi regime.)

War raged between the Germans and the Russians throughout the occupation. The Germans pushed deep into Russia, but
gradually they got beaten back. By late summer 1944 the front
was rapidly moving west. Jakobīne and Jānis knew it was only
a matter of time before the Russians once again overran their
country.

The Russian Air Force identified the family's house as a military target because of the communications center in the basement. In October 1944, in the middle of the night, first one,
then another earth-ripping, house-shaking explosions tossed
John and the other occupants of his house out of their beds.
The Russians had bombed the house. No one was injured, but
the next morning Ivars and John stood in the garden gaping at
two two-foot-long conical craters with radiating striations so
close to the house that shrapnel had ripped holes up and down
the parlor wall.

The attack frightened John's parents, Jānis especially. The
Germans living in their house, Jānis's job working for the Reich:
though these circumstances were not of their choosing, Jānis
and Jakobīne realized that when the Russians arrived, they

would be identified as Nazi collaborators. The family considered escaping to Sweden on one of the hundreds of small boats ferrying people across the open sea from Riga to Stockholm in the dead of night, a distance of 275 miles. Jakobīne's older sister and her family had made this journey, arriving in Sweden with nothing but the clothes on their backs.

The German military had begun withdrawing men and material by sea across the Baltic to Poland. Latvian civilians willing to work for the regime were allowed to travel with them. One of the Wehrmacht soldiers suggested that John's family could find refuge living with his parents in their tiny village in the Sudetenland, a German-controlled enclave on the Czech–German border. This invitation carried weight, and the necessary papers allowing them to travel were soon obtained. Jakobīne had been preparing for this escape for some time. In her possession: two huge wooden crates that she packed with as many of the family's belongings as would fit—winter clothing; bed linens; pots and pans; precious family papers and photos, including the deeds to the family's house in Lielvārde and the Riga apartment building; plus many medicinal compounds that she had squirrelled away.

And that's not all. Early in the war Jakobīne had stockpiled liters of safe, potable hundred-proof grain alcohol. Cut with water, grain alcohol turned into vodka, a substance more valuable than gold during wartime when soldiers seeking surcease from their misery drank anything, everything: gasoline, perfume, turpentine, all deadly. (American sailors in the Pacific mixed pineapple juice with torpedo fuel containing grain alcohol and called it Torpedo Juice.) Jakobīne nailed the crates closed. Jānis wheeled them to the railroad station, where he paid for them to be shipped by rail to the Sudetenland address.

Jānis's bachelor friend, Edwards, the sweet-natured veteran whom the children called Uncle though he was no relation, traveled with them. Jānis Senior's mother, the children's grandmother who was in her eighties, remained behind. Before leaving Riga, Jānis Senior took his younger son to visit Riga's beloved Freedom Monument. This tall, slender art deco structure located on the edge of medieval Old Town had been erected less than ten years before to honor Latvian soldiers killed during the 1918 war of independence. Standing before the monument, Jānis tearfully told his son that he feared he would never see his homeland again, and indeed, he did not.

15. Mrs. Abel

John was five and a half years old. His expression was solemn, his blond hair had been shorn to prevent lice, exposing his pale scalp. Silently he stood in the parlor in Lielvārde dressed in knee socks, leather shoes with straps, scratchy woolen short pants, and a stiff starched white linen shirt, also itchy, but in a different way. Ever since two Russian bombs fell from the sky, the household has been in an uproar. His parents told him the family must run away.

For John leaving meant just one thing. Leaving his nanny, Mrs. Abel.

"But Mama, why can't she come with us?" he asked again and again.

"We have no room," his mother answered.

"She can fit in my valise," John said.

"We have no room," his mother repeated. "Even grandmother must stay behind."

He didn't believe he could be parted from Mrs. Abel.

It wouldn't happen.

It couldn't happen.

He squirmed getting dressed. "Hurry up, Jāni. Hurry up," his mother said impatiently. He stood on the rug in the parlor in his scratchy clothes looking down at the rug's swirling dark patterns.

"Say goodbye to Mrs. Abel," his mother said.

"Give her a hug," his mother said.

"Go on, Jāni. Give her a hug, you might never see her again," his father said gruffly.

John stood still as a statue. If he didn't move, if he didn't breathe, if he didn't speak, maybe time would stop. Mrs. Abel bent down and put her arms around him. He longed to put his arms around her, but he didn't do it. He held his breath and pretended she wasn't there. She wasn't there. He wasn't there. She wasn't there. Say goodbye. Say goodbye. Say goodbye.

Soon she was gone. Soon they were gone. Not one tear trickled down his nose. (To this day John responds to change—good change and bad—with a blank face. Our wedding photographer, noting his lack of obvious emotion, asked at our reception, "What's with John?" At the time, I didn't understand that in moments of high emotion John's face was expressionless. Eventually I figured out that when flooded with feeling, John froze. Later he would process whatever dramatic event—our marriage, the birth of our son, the birth of our grandchildren—had just occurred and the fluidity of his emotions would be restored.)

16. Cargo Ship and First Train

In Riga, the family boarded a German cargo ship bound for the Polish port the Germans called Danzig (Gdańsk in Polish). Crowded into the ship's triple-decker hold were hundreds of filthy, starving Russian prisoners of war dressed in rags, on their way to almost certain death in German slave labor camps. Higher up, on the top two decks, Latvian refugees swathed in layers of heavy clothing sat or reclined on their valises during the three-day Baltic crossing. The Russian Air Force—unaware or unconcerned about the prisoners—bombed the ship but missed.

From Danzig the family traveled on a series of trains across Poland to the German-controlled part of Czechoslovakia known as the Sudetenland. Numerous times the Russians bombed the trains on which they traveled—again they missed. On the German–Czech border, in the little town of Niedergrund (the Czechs later renamed it Dolní Podluží), the kindly parents of the Wehrmacht soldier who had offered them refuge welcomed John and his family into their home. Thanks to the efficiency of the German National Railway, the crates full of their belongings arrived a few weeks later. Nazi authorities put Jānis Senior and Edwards to work salvaging parts from downed military aircraft. For a while, the family was safe.

17. What Is Not Known Cannot Be Remembered

In John's version of the story, the Russian airmen who bombed his house in Lielvārde and attacked the ship on which the family sailed and the trains on which they traveled were, to recall the title of the comic novel, members of an aerial gang who couldn't shoot straight. This belief is false: late in the war, the Russian Air Force killed tens of thousands of soldiers and civilians. John's understanding of the risk he and his family faced when he was a child does not reflect what he knows as an educated adult about risk and probability. It expresses, instead, a small child's perception of his own invincibility. Having come through unscathed, John "knows" this is how his story was destined to unfold. He cannot process or will not process information to the contrary. While survivors sometimes bear witness to catastrophic violence, often they do not. Survivors' minds, and our minds in general, prefer to falsify. We humans love a happy ending. We are hardwired to generalize from our own experience, and in doing this, we often distort history.

18. Leaving the Sudentenland

For six months, as the front moved inexorably toward them, the family remained in the Sudetenland. In February, with the Red Army only days away, Jakobīne and Jānis knew they must flee once again. I suspect some portion of Jakobīne's stash of grain alcohol convinced a German bureaucrat to give the family and a small group of Latvian companions a cattle car in which to escape west. (Having carried millions of Hitler's victims east to their deaths, a glut of these cars sat empty on German rail crossings at the end of the war. Ironic that one of these cars, the mobile apotheosis of death, was offered as a means of delivering John and his family to safety.) Sometime before they left Niedergrund, John's family learned that the soldiers who ran the communications center in the basement of their house had been sent to the Eastern front. The enlisted man whose parents welcomed them so warmly never returned home.

The cattle car, with ten inhabitants and all their belongings, traveled southwest across Germany hooked to a coal train that, due to its valuable cargo, was directed and perhaps protected by the German military. To avoid Allied attack, the coal train traveled mostly at night. More than once when they arrived at a rail depot, come morning's light, they discovered that it had been bombed. John remembers seeing railroad tracks jutting crazily into the sky. At war's end only 10 percent of Germany's railroads were operating. On at least one occasion John remembers watching a heavily bombed city burning in the night. Despite the February cold, the car was warmish and stuffy, probably due to a small coal stove. John's mother spread blankets on top of the family's wooden crates and that's where they slept. A toilet was hidden in a corner, separated by a curtain. To pass the time, the occupants sang, accompanied by a woman playing the accordion. John especially liked a sentimental World War II love song called "The Blue Headscarf."

When they stopped, John's parents climbed down from the cattle car and went in search of food. John believes it was his German-speaking father who managed to find provisions. Ivars credits their mother, who may still have had small quantities of grain alcohol and medical compounds to trade. Together the two made certain that their family had enough to eat as they traveled slowly south and west to safety.

John's wartime childhood certainly traumatized him. Living with him, I know that to be the case. Still, his parents did a heroic job protecting themselves and their sons. John was young enough (Ivars was not) to believe in his parents' invincibility.

Early in March the cattle car rolled into the small city of Ravensburg, located near Lake Constance, not far from the Swiss border. Neighbors from Lielvārde had written to John's parents when they were living in Niedergrund suggesting that they head in this direction, far from any major military targets. As their neighbors had predicted, Allied bombers had largely spared Ravensburg, which was home to the famed maker of wooden toys and puzzles called Ravensburger Spieleverlag, a Swiss-operated Red Cross supply center, and very little else. Like the doves released by Noah after the flood, Jānis Senior and Uncle, rucksacks on their backs, climbed down from the cattle car, looked around, then took off on foot in search of a bit of dry land where they might settle. Eventually they arrived in the small town of Ebenweiler, twenty kilometers (twelve miles) from the railroad station, where Uncle found a job in a lumberyard. Someone in town told the travelers that the surrounding villages, depleted of men, were in desperate need of farm labor. Jānis trekked a mile and a half down a dirt road from Ebenweiler to Egg.

19. War's End

On May 4, 1945, in the hamlet of Egg, John, who was five and a half years old, stood barefoot and alert in his landlord's yard, watching World War II roll to a close. White sheets, signaling surrender, hung from all the houses strung along the village's meandering dirt road. A bedraggled German soldier on a bicycle—hat comically askew—raised a cloud of dust as he raced westward up the hill on the far side of the village. For a short while, that undignified figure with his urgent pedaling defined the western front. Then a band of French soldiers strode down the other side of the hill and into the village. Their presence announced that, in this tiny dot of a place, the war was over.

Herr Kazenheimer's farm—he was their landlord—was set apart on a spur on the high point of the road running through the village. The French conquerors, led by a Colonel Heydar dressed in a pressed uniform with a revolver at his hip and a German shepherd at his heel, arrived at Kazenheimer's house first. Following the colonel were a half dozen conscripts from the French colony of Mali, carrying rifles, heavy packs on their backs. The men's skin was as black as the nighttime sky. The villagers gaped. Most had never seen an African.

Without asking permission, the colonel and his men entered Kazenheimer's stucco farmhouse, emerging a few minutes later.

"Who lives in this house?" the colonel asked in well-schooled German.

Speaking in the local dialect, Kazenheimer conveyed that he owned the farm and the house and that he and Frau Kazenheimer and four *ausländer* from *Lettland* lived here as well. (He made no mention of the picture of Hitler his wife had hastily torn from the wall and hidden under their bed.)

"Any men of fighting age living in this house?" The officer asked.

"Nein."

"Any men of fighting age in this village?"

"Nein."

"Any weapons stored here?"

"Nein."

"Any munitions?"

"Nein." (Kazenheimer kept silent about the live grenades and other ordnance scattered about in the nearby woods. These explosives had rained down on the area a few days earlier, after the German army blew up a munitions train outside of Eibenweiler to prevent German explosives from falling into Allied hands.)

"Any large stores of grain and food?"

"Nein." (All crops beyond subsistence had been requisitioned in the fall by the Reich.)

"Any gasoline?"

"Nein."

"Any printing press?"

"Nein."

As the colonel questioned their landlord, John stared in wonderment at the French soldiers. What set them apart as much as their color was the way they stood. These were soldiers without the tensed shoulders, stiff necks, tight jaws, and ramrod posture of German military men. Covered in grime and obviously fatigued, they looked comfortable in their own skins, their body language resembling that of the American GIs who later visited the area.

The questioning was over.

What would happen next?

The villagers held their breaths.

One of the French soldiers picked up his rifle and took aim. A shot rang out in the yard, blowing the head off a chicken. Another shot rang out. Another dead chicken. Soon a cooking fire blazed in Kazenheimer's yard. The villagers watched silently as the troops sat down under a tree to eat their meal. Soon the colonel gave a sign and the soldiers rose, gathered up their gear and left the yard. After stopping to look around two other farms, they marched up the hill on the far side of the village and were gone. The war was over, and in this little corner of Germany, the free French were in charge. (Three days later, on May 7, the German high command unconditionally surrendered all of the German armies to the Western Allies.)

20. Flashbulb Memories

That scene—John standing barefoot watching World War II roll to a close—didn't come from a photograph and I didn't make it up. The German soldier, his hat tilted perilously, and his cloud of dust, those French infantrymen "black as night," the shots ringing out, the dead chickens: John remembers all of this and much more. When describing these events, he always includes the same details and uses the same language.

For years I wondered about John's photographic recall of childhood events. Where did it come from? I knew John to be a very visual person. In everyday life, he saw and remembered details others, including me, overlooked, but that explanation didn't seem to go far enough. When I stumbled upon a description of "flashbulb memories," I thought I might have found a deeper truth. According to a theory proposed by a pair of psychologists in 1977, flashbulb memories capture dramatic—often traumatic—events. Like moments caught in a camera's flash, they are said to be accurate and detailed, but cut loose from context and emotions. Unlike other forms of memory, flashbulb memories are said to retain their immediacy and accuracy over time. This description seemed to pertain to John, but I could not be sure. Recent studies of survivors of the 9/11 attacks have undermined the belief that flashbulb memories are immutable. Like other forms of memory, these memories do change over time, although they may change less than other forms of memory. As to John, I do not know how or why his memories remain so intact. Nor do I know if my writing about his life, and his reading what I have written about his life, has altered what he knows and what he remembers.

21. Oberschwaben

The Appalachia of Germany. That's how John described Oberschwaban (Upper Swabia), the remote corner of southwest Germany where Egg is located, and where his family watched the war draw to a close. In Egg they lived among farmers who could not read and write and whose knowledge of the world scarcely extended beyond their village. (Although German physicians knew for a century that consuming iodized salt prevented goiter, a condition causing the thyroid to swell, many women in the area suffered from this unsightly malady.) The locals among whom John lived spoke an extreme version of the Swabian dialect that other Germans found hilarious, and they adhered to a form of Catholicism that recalled the Middle Ages. The local priest thundered his condemnation of bathing from the pulpit, saying it glorified nakedness and was sinful. Equally abhorrent to this prelate was the Latvian fondness for swimming in nearby ponds and lakes.

22. French Zone Food

Whatever military liberated you—English, French, American, or (God forbid) Russian—that was the zone you inhabited, and that country was responsible for taking care of you and providing you with food and shelter. (The Russians didn't feed and house. They sent refugees home labeled as traitors to face consequences that might result in a fast death by bullet or a slower death in the gulag.) Since the French Provisional government was broke, they handed off the job of feeding and housing refugees to the local German farmers under their control.

This meant that many displaced persons in the French zone lived in real houses, not barracks, and they ate fresh food. Virtually all other DPs lived communally, and they ate what was readily available. Refugees in the American zone ate canned food. Refugees in the French zone were not exempt from the famine that plagued all of Europe after the war, when farmers had no seed, no fertilizer, and no fuel, and weather conditions were the worst in a century. John remembers that his father, who had been quite stout, lost so much weight he and his younger son could both fit in his prewar pants. Still, they were better off than most, receiving rotating supplies of potatoes, carrots, cabbage, spelt, oats, wheat, apples, pears, berries, and sugar beet, plus small amounts of meat and dairy, from local farmers. (Cut off from and somewhat hostile to the Nazi state, Swabian farmers most likely had hidden livestock and seed from Nazi requisitioners, hence their ability to feed themselves and the refugees living among them immediately following the war.)

To supplement what they were given by their neighbors, John's family foraged in the woods for mushrooms, berries, dandelions, and other wild greens; walnuts, chestnuts, and beechnuts, no bigger than a pinky nail, from which Oma squeezed droplets of oil—fat was in the shortest supply. (John's German friend Gert told us that after the war, his mother refused to throw out beechnut oil stored in a glass container into which a mouse had crawled, died, and decayed. Mouse-infused cooking oil was better than none.) Before the war ended, John's father earned the family's keep by working in Kazenheimer's fields. After the war, the family even gleaned, gathering up stray shafts of grain, just like in the bible.

As to bread: Once the international rescue effort (largely paid for by the Americans) was fully launched, the United Nations Relief and Rehabilitation Administration (UNRRA), delivered large rounds of German multigrained bread to Eibenweiler weekly for distribution among the many Latvian families living in the vicinity. Due to word of mouth and the purported fondness of the local French commandant for his Latvian mistress, the region surrounding Ebenweiler had attracted many Latvian refugees and was designated an official Latvian Displaced Persons camp. (The French, with their own issues related to wartime complicity, did not automatically assume the worst of the many Latvians who had been conscripted and sent to the Eastern front to fight the Russians.) Because he got along with every clique and faction, John's father was elected leader of the camp, a job requiring him to oversee the distribution of the bread and other supplies provided by UNRRA. "Not as good as *our* bread" is how Ivars remembers the United Nations rye bread. "But it was okay. Sufficient."

Neither John nor Ivars experienced their family's years in Germany through the lens of extreme hunger or breadlessness. Anxiety about the future plagued the family—where would they go? What was to become of them?—but they did not suffer the psychic or physical wounds of starvation, and the absence of Latvian rye bread did not tantalize or torment them. Not until the early 1950s when they were living in Butler, Pennsylvania, four miles from the nearest Latvian family, did they experience that profound sense of loss and longing. Ironically, it was in America—not Germany—where, regarding bread, they were the most displaced. And it was there in Pennsylvania, on the western side of the Atlantic, that John's mother taught herself to bake Latvian rye bread.

23. British Zone Food

The United States could have alleviated the monumental famine that swept across Europe if it had behaved in 1945 and 1946 as it had in 1918, when it provided massive amounts of food relief. Part of the problem was bureaucratic. The UNRRA, an organization largely funded by the US government but not entirely answerable to it, dissipated control and responsibility. Moreover, after years of government requisitioning and price controls, American farmers were eager to return to profitability, and the American public had lost its patience with rationing and restraint. Rather than sending surplus grain to Europe and Japan to feed starving populations, these commodities were fed to chicken, hogs, and cattle for domestic consumption. America feasted in the postwar years while millions elsewhere continued to go hungry. Blame this oversight on a failure of imagination. That so much suffering could follow so much suffering was unfathomable in a land where no bombs fell, no battles were fought, and death by starvation was virtually unknown. Maija Krustāns Šlesers, John's friend and fellow refugee, whose family spent five years in the British zone after the war, experienced the postwar famine far more viscerally than John. She later described her experience to me in great detail. Her memories resemble those recorded by Marta Hillers, a young German diarist living in Berlin at war's end: "All thinking and feeling, all wishes and hopes began with food." Sustaining Maija during her coldest, darkest hours: the lingering memory of her grandmother Kristine's *rupjmaize*.

24. Geography Is Destiny 2

Maija Krustāns and her family left Latvia on a ship bound for Poland in the fall of 1944, same as John and his family. But her family's experience sailing into Gotenhafen ("Gdynia," in Polish) was very different from John's. Arriving in Gotenhafen, the Krustāns family then traveled by rail 120 miles south, to a small city in Poland called *Toruń*, located due east of Berlin. Due east of Berlin was not a good place to be at the end of the war. While John's family spent about a week traveling across Germany in a cattle car, the Krustānses' trek mostly on foot from *Toruń* northwest to Lübeck, a German city in what became the British zone, while only slightly longer, took four months, during which starvation, exposure, trauma, and death accompanied them every foot of the way.

25. Maija: The Journey

In late January, with *Toruń's* fall to the Russians imminent and snow blanketing all of Poland, Maija's uncle, a skilled technician, used scrap metal to build a sled with metal runners on which the family was able to pile some of their belongings, including a few precious books.

"The Russians were coming. We had to get out," Maija recalled, adding there was no time to buy food. Heading north and west, they had little to eat except pocket-sized pieces of hard-toasted rye bread that Maija's grandmother Kristīne had stuffed into a large linen pillowcase six months earlier when the family left Riga. (As a refugee fleeing Latvia during World War I, Kristīne had learned firsthand the life-sustaining value of such a gift.) As was the Latvian custom, Maija's grandmother baked the bread, sliced it into cracker-sized pieces, and toasted it in the oven until it was almost hard enough to crack teeth, then presented it as a parting gift to her family. In this form, rye bread lasts for years. The family had no need for Kristīne's *rupjmaize* until February 1945, when, Maija says with great feeling, "It saved our bodies and our souls."

"On the first day of our escape, we walked thirty kilometers. It was so cold. My mother bundled us up in double mittens and double shawls and she stuffed pieces of granny's bread in our coat pockets. I ate snow to moisten the bread. I remember sucking on each piece, letting it slowly melt in my mouth as if it were chocolate."

The bridge across the Vistula River had been blown up. "My uncle pulled the sled over the frozen river. We didn't know how thick the ice was. We made it across, but the ice gave way in places and people drowned." Others were fished out of the water by the Russians and sent back.

After crossing the river, the family walked for many days. The dried rye bread staved off their hunger until they arrived in a village where they were able to purchase supplies and could sleep in an abandoned farmhouse.

"When we ran out of rye bread, we shook the last crumbs from the pillowcase and ate them. Then for a long time all we had to eat was a bag of dried oatmeal."

They traveled by rail when they could. "I remember sitting on a train, across from a very young German soldier who had a loaf of white bread. He could see we were starving, and he tore off a piece and gave it to us."

On their journey west, the family slept in little German *Dörfer* ("villages"). Once, when Maija's mother and uncle were out searching for food, the area where they were staying was heavily bombarded by the Allies. Bombs exploded around them, making a terrifying racket. The house where they were staying was hit. Maija and her brother were not hurt, but they were traumatized. "When the grown-ups returned, we could not speak. We shook with fear. I still have nightmares," she says. (Seventy-five years later, Maija describes herself as suffering still from post-traumatic stress disorder.)

They walked on cratered roads where units had engaged in combat, exposed to sights too horrifying for her to share. What Maija does describe are the dead and dying horses injured by shrapnel and bombs while pulling artillery carts and other heavy equipment. "The horses were struggling to get up, struggling to escape their harnesses. When I petted them, I could hear that gargling sound in their throats that dying animals make. I whispered in their ears that it was going to be all right. They were so beautiful, those horses." (Dead or dying, they would soon be butchered for their meat.)

Day after day, week after week, month after month, snowstorm after snowstorm, they walked across Germany. Food that winter was so scarce, the family ate potato peelings. Frightened and cold, they trudged on.

When she told me this story, Maija was a frail old woman. That once in wartime, in winter, she had the strength to walk across Europe: this memory rendered her incredulous. Where had she had gotten the strength?, she asked. And then she remembered. The conviction that a better life awaited them: that hope, persisting beyond all reason, had kept them in motion. "We were like wild birds flying blindly to the west," she told me.

The snow melted. Spring made its appearance. Maija's uncle found an abandoned Volkswagen in the woods where the family had taken refuge. He dismantled its wrecked frame, using the rims and tires to create a cart with functional wheels. Pushing this makeshift cart through the forest, they heard that the war would soon be over. "Uncle chopped down a small tree. He tore up a white sheet and tied it to the pole. . . . My little brother sat on top of the wagon holding onto our white flag."

Leaving the safety of the forest, they arrived in Lübeck. "We stopped at the first house we came to. My mother couldn't walk another step." An elderly German woman lived in the house with her daughter and her daughter's children. The old woman questioned Maija's mother and uncle. "When she learned we came from Riga, she invited us to stay."

The date was May 8, 1945. VE Day. Victory in Europe Day. The day the Allies formally accepted Nazi Germany's unconditional surrender. The war was over. The Russian military would move no farther west. Maija and her family had made it to the West with no days to spare.

They stayed with the German family for a year. The old lady and her family were kind. Maija and her brother played with the other children in the house and Maija was allowed to play the family's piano. To satisfy their omnipresent hunger, they picked wild sorrel and nettles and gathered mushrooms in the forest. With these meager ingredients they made soup flavored with bits of mustard and other ingredients stored in little jars in their host's larder.

Another Latvian woman, a little younger than Maija, remembers her mother sending her to the butcher shop immediately after the war with an aluminum milk can to beg the butcher to give her the water in which he had boiled sausage.

Her mother used that water flavored with a bead or two of fat to make soup. Food like this is more imaginary than real. This Latvian girl was not so different from Marta Hillers in Berlin, who wrote that hunger at the end of the war drove her to run her finger again and again over words in a novel describing a fancy meal, as if the words themselves could nourish.

Eventually, British authorities arranged for the Krustāns family to move into a Displaced Persons camp for Latvian refugees, where Maija and her brother could go to school and where their mother, a schoolteacher in Latvia, once again could teach. In the camp the family lived in a barracks, crowded into a single room. Day after day the British, flat broke themselves and facing severe food shortages at home, served the refugees a kind of porridge made from dried peas and lentils. Everyone called it the green horror. "Just thinking about it, my stomach turns over," Maija recalls. Tiny garden plots for growing vegetables helped, as did additional support arriving from the US, UNRRA, and the International Rescue Committee (IRC).

In 1950 Maija's family found an American sponsor and moved to Baltimore. The family lived in a small apartment building on North Avenue with several other refugee families. Maija went to school and excelled. Eventually she won scholarships, but Baltimore bewildered her. Ladies from the Lutheran Church delivered used hats and white nylon gloves that they insisted Maija and her mother wear to church on Sunday. Race relations in Baltimore shocked them—"I was berated for sitting with Black people in the back of the bus," Maija recalls. The horrible American bread with its weird nonfoodlike consistency filled them with an existential loneliness. "On top of the building where we lived was a huge billboard advertising Wonder Bread. It seemed fitting."

26. A Gendered Point of View

Up to a point, Maija can talk about the ways in which violence and privation traumatized her. Not John. John describes his family's wartime dislocation in filmic detail as if it were a great adventure. He never speaks of fear. Or homesickness. To protect themselves and their parents, Ivars and John learned to suppress their emotions and their personal desires. They learned not to ask for what their parents could not provide: doing so, John said, would have been disloyal. The only feeling John refers to when talking about the war is his mother's anxiety concerning their family's future. Yes, the family was physically unscathed during their journeys across Europe. Yes, time and again the bombs falling in their vicinity failed to hit their target. Still, as a small child John traveled through a world on fire. I can't help wondering if he would feel compelled to tell his story time and again if the language of emotion had been accessible to him then? And if the language of emotion had been accessible to him, would his inner life still be divided into bipolar chambers in which on one side feelings are suppressed and on the other they run amok? I ponder, too, the impact of his mother's gendered ideas on John's development. Oma believed in the intrinsic superiority of traditionally male attributes such as silence, forbearance, and stoicism. For her and for her eldest son, and sometimes for her youngest, her husband Jānis Senior's expressions of emotion (his joy came easily; his anger came easily, too) were a sign of an unmanly weakness. Real men, serious men, kept their mouths shut.

27. Their House

After surveying the housing stock in Egg, the French administrator moved John's family out of Herr Kazenheimer's house into the larger quarters of Frau Ringeburger, a war widow with two children. The house was one story. John's family lived in the right half. Mrs. R, with her two children, lived in the left half. The shared kitchen was in the middle, with a wood-burning stove and a water pump. There was no central heat and no bathroom, only an outhouse, attached to the house, but the village had electricity. All the houses had power, but light bulbs were as scarce as gasoline. None could be bought or bartered. When a light bulb burned out, Ivars rotated and gently jiggled it until the broken filament made contact. As electricity flowed the filament welded itself, providing light in the living room. (Most amazing to me in this story: six-year-old John's powers of observation.) Oma sent John to the woods to collect firewood. The Duke of Württenberg owned the forest—John sometimes saw him driving through the village in a white BMW convertible, a prewar model. The duke also owned the ponds and the fish in the ponds, although John and Mrs. Ringeburger's son Heinz, who was just a little older, fished in the ponds anyway. John's parents were amused to hear their youngest speaking Swabian with Heinz—John was the only one in his family who mastered the local dialect.

Frau Ringeburger raised chickens and gave John's family eggs. John's parents planted a small garden and raised rabbits for meat. The mama rabbit was John's pet. A black-and-white photo in a family album shows John cradling a large white rabbit with distinctive black spots, his expression serious and tender. Eventually, Oma slaughtered his pet, although she honored his refusal to eat the creature he had loved. (As an adult, John reacts to this memory with characteristic contrariness, relishing the chance to tell our guests, children included, that his mother served his pet for supper.)

28. A Singular Boyhood

John's rapscallion boyhood recalls Huck Finn. He blew his nose on his sleeve and rarely wore shoes. He climbed slender tree branches high above the earth. He and Heinz roamed the woods. They had a taste for pranks that ended badly. His father's switch swinging by the door spoke to mischief gone awry. He bathed once a week in a bathtub in the kitchen filled with water heated for the occasion—all four of members of his family used the same water. His was a childhood far less deprived than that of most Latvian exiles his age, many of whom lived in crowded barracks without any of the comforts of home. It was, however, a childhood few Americans, including his children, could comprehend.

29. The Family Dynamic

His mother told him things about his father that he did not want to hear. He could see his mother's point—Oma wanted Jānis Senior to learn English and take other steps to prepare for the family's future in a new land. John's father, who got along with everyone, had been elected to lead their non-camp

camp, comprised of forty or fifty families living in and around
Ebenweiler, half of whom despised the other. His main job: dis-
tributing food and donated clothing. The post came with a little office. Most days Jānis Senior could be found playing cards
there with his buddies, which infuriated Oma. John found
himself going back and forth between his parents: siding in his
mind with his father when his mother made cutting comments,
siding with his mother when his father's heedlessness seemed to
go too far. When the family dynamic overwhelmed John, there
was always Uncle Edwards, who visited on weekends. Uncle
had no agenda. He didn't vie for John's love. Together John
and Uncle would lie in the grass and watch the ants or Uncle
would talk to him about geography. When the family thought
they would be settling in Australia, as many Latvian families
did, Uncle arrived with a small world atlas to show John a picture of the giant continent on the other side of the world where
someday they hoped to live.

30. School

At six and a half, John enrolled in the newly organized Latvian
school in Fronhofen, a town five kilometers (three miles) away
from Egg, where he was taught by exiles who had been teachers
in Latvia. There was no transportation. He walked both ways
with Ivars, who attended the Latvian upper school in the same
town. Subjects were taught in Latvian. Students also learned
French and some English. German wasn't taught, although
most of the refugees spoke some German. As was the tradition, several grades gathered in a single classroom. John, who
had been solving math problems with his father for as long as

he could remember, proved himself to be a math whiz. When teachers in the higher grades posed questions—multiplication, division, that sort of thing—John, without thinking, would call out the answer.

Eventually, the lower school and the Latvian high school moved to Ebenweiler, making life easier for John and Ivars.

31. Crucifixion

Schools in Germany were church-affiliated, either Protestant or Catholic, and religion was a required subject. (Latvian schools were associated with the Latvian Lutheran Church.) At Easter, when John was in the second grade, his teacher described the crucifixion, focusing on the gory parts. Our Lord's flayed skin. The nails piercing his precious hands and feet. The blood spurting from his wounds. Moreover, his teacher told the class, her tone grave and utterly sincere, the suffering of Jesus was nothing compared to the torture they as sinners would endure in hell for all eternity.

John took this lesson very seriously. He imagined himself being burned alive. He thought about his hair bursting into flame like dry kindling and his body blackening like a rabbit turning on a spit. He lay in bed at night fearing he would die in his sleep and wake up burning in hell. His father tried to reassure him, suggesting that when he was older, he would understand more and could decide for himself what he thought. His father was right. As a young teenager John decided that a religion based on torture was an abomination. He dared God to strike him dead for this heretical thought, and when that didn't happen, he slammed the door shut on Christianity and locked it tight.

32. The Dentist

One of John's upper teeth was growing inward instead of straight up and down. A German dentist in Ravensburg had the skill to fix it. To reach the dentist, John and his father rode a wood-burning bus. (Only the Allied troops had gasoline, and they weren't sharing with civilians, especially German civilians.) A wood-burning metal cylinder replaced the bus's gasoline engine. This device produced enough power to propel the bus forward on the straightaway. Hills were another matter. Approaching an incline, the driver would do his best to gain momentum. He would make it two thirds of the way up and then the bus would roll to a stop. At this point John remembers the bus driver standing up and shouting, "*Ala passageiria aussteigen*," Swabian for "Everybody out of the bus." (This phrase, remembered and translated by John, made a deep impression. Prior to exiting the car, his children grew up hearing their dad bark, "*Ala passageiria aussteigen!*" with the last three syllables, *aushh, sty gen*, spit out for dramatic effect.) As to John's childhood adventure: With a lightened load and the passengers pushing, the wood-burning stove was able to produce sufficient oomph to get to the top of the hill. Going downhill, no problem. Passengers could once again hop aboard.

Not a perfect way to travel. But it got them where they were going. The dentist jerry-rigged a retainer for John's tooth and within six months it was pointing in the right direction.

33. Stuff

There was nothing to buy and no money to buy it. The German currency was worthless and remained so until the deutsche mark was introduced in June 1948. There was the black market—teachers in parts of Germany were paid in black-market cigarettes. Simple household objects could not be replaced and were therefore cherished. A linen tablecloth, a paring knife, sewing needles, these were treasures. John's discovery of a tin plate in the woods meant something and his cleverness fixing things earned him praise. A prized possession to this day: the small paring knife with the wooden handle he repaired for his mother by inserting three copper rivets.

34. Pyromania

One summer afternoon John and Heinz walked to the village where the German military had blown up its munitions train at the end of the war. John had a few coins Uncle had given him for his birthday. The boys sauntered into a beer garden and ordered a pint of beer—goodbye to all of John's money. Feeling very big, the boys drank the beer. Then they went to the woods to reconnoiter. They poked around in the underbrush looking for explosives. They found a box outfitted with balsa wood in which a dozen holes had been drilled. In each hole: an intact dynamite detonating cap. What could be more thrilling? They carried their booty home and hid it. A few days later when the grown-ups were out of the house, the boys put a dynamite detonating cap in Frau Ringeburger's stove, the one that heated her living room and bedroom. If one cap was good, two, of course, was better, so they added a second cap. When Frau Ringeburger lit the stove, a glorious blast of ground-shaking noise erupted and the stovepipe flew off. Blast number two erupted just as noisily, filling the room with waves of soot and dust. Soot in their eyes. Soot in their hair. Soot all over the walls and the bed and the sofa and the curtains.

Both boys got a beating for their prank. John didn't mind because he knew he was guilty. Besides, a beating was nothing compared to the thrill of blowing up the house.

35. Stilts

John and Heinz built stilts from materials they nicked and scavenged from nearby farms and fields. The standing platforms of the first pairs were above their knees. They got so skilled at maneuvering, they could hop up and down on a single stilt as if it were a pogo stick. Next came stilts with platforms at the level of their heads. There was a masonry porch in front of the house with a set of stairs on each side. To launch themselves, they stood on the porch and fell forward. Which was scary. Finally, they built stilts two or three feet above their heads. These required standing on the porch railing and diving. To dismount they crossed the road and fell into the embankment. Both boys got so skilled they could walk up the stairs on one side of the landing and down the other set.

When John's family left Germany and moved to Pennsylvania, stilts became his calling card at his new school. He would stand on the playground on his homemade stilts and kids would ride their bikes through his legs. Up on his stilts he wasn't just the new kid, the foreigner, he was one of the gang. At home, standing on his stilts, he cleaned the gutters for his mother.

The adventure of it all, the independence, the mastery of new skills—freedom such as this came to define boyhood for him.

36. The First Time He Thought About Suicide

His father had a taste for luxury, and a taste for sweets. Somehow, he had managed to get his hands on a stash of fine chocolate. He squirreled the chocolate away. But then the candy went missing. His father searched everywhere. Thievery was the only explanation.

He accused John of taking the candy.

John insisted that he had not.

His father did not believe him.

His father retrieved a menacing tri-pronged rubber gasket, one that had fallen out of the back of an army truck. He grabbed his son and pulled down his pants. He whaled on John, insisting he confess.

John wouldn't confess. His refusals fueled his father's anger. Stroke followed stroke, until John confessed to a crime that he had not committed.

He had ugly red welts on his legs and buttocks.

The invisible wounds were worse.

He was ashamed to be seen.

He wouldn't leave the house.

He wouldn't go swimming.

His mood became sadder and sadder.

He decided he would kill himself. He would throw himself in front of one of the military trucks that periodically rumbled down the road in front of his house. Or he would stick a wire in the electric outlet and electrocute himself.

He stayed inside, brooding.

Eventually his mother asked him what was wrong.

"I didn't take that candy," John cried, bursting into tears and throwing himself into his mother's arms.

She believed him. So he didn't have to die.

Still, the wound caused by his father's injustice lingered. He loved his father so much. Which made the betrayal so much worse.

37. Injustice

Probably John's father ate the chocolates and didn't remember. His father was like that. Unquestioning of his own virtue.

38. Der Teufel

After the family had been living in Egg for three or four years, the local Swabians had begun muttering about those blood-sucking Ausländers they were required to house and feed. In this embittered atmosphere, Swabian teens began picking fights with young Latvians. The Latvians were outnumbered. Ivars was beaten up more than once. When other Latvian boys did not come to his rescue, Ivars made himself a pair of brass knuckles.

It was summer. John, having imbibed his brother's seething anger and no doubt possessing some of his own, was sitting by himself on the side of the lake in Ebenweiler watching three young Germans roughhousing in the water. The guys worked at the sawmill and were on their lunch break. John had seen them cross the road, drop their lunch pails on the grassy shore, and strip down to their long johns, baring muscled chests and arms. He envied their freedom.

One of the Germans looked up and caught John watching him and his friends. He was handsome. With black hair, a broad forehead, and a full mouth. A scar as thick and twisty as rope ran up his right arm from the elbow to the shoulder.

"What's your name, kid?" the German guy asked in Swabian.

John understood the question, but he didn't answer. Silent defiance. That was his style.

"What's your name, kid?" the man repeated.

John looked in his direction. "*Der Teufel*," he answered. The devil.

The German guy clambered onto the grass to confront John, who was small for his age and skinny. Water dripped from his body. "What's your name?" he repeated.

John was scared, but he wouldn't give in. "*Der Teufel*," he repeated.

The man grabbed John's shoulders and pinned him to the ground. "What's your name?" he shouted.

John was a younger brother. He'd been body locked and overpowered before. Instead of answering, he spat in the German guy's face.

With a roar the man picked John up and hurled him, fully dressed, into the lake.

John's father and his friends were playing cards farther down the side of the lake. They looked up and saw John flailing in the water. John's father hoisted himself up. "What's going on?" he inquired, taking in the scene. John climbed out of the water. He had nothing to say.

39. Leaving Egg

The resettlement process took years. The United States stayed out of it at first, allowing countries in need of skilled labor such as Australia and Venezuela to have first dibs on the refugees. John and his family watched many of the Latvian families in their camp depart for Australia, hoping, expecting, that they, too, would be chosen. But they were not. The Australian government rejected their resettlement application, deeming John's father too old (he was sixty), and his sons too young to contribute any time soon to Australia's postwar economy. Late in 1948, the United States government began accepting refugees unwanted by other nations so long as they were sponsored by organizations that had sufficient contacts and enough money to guarantee paid employment to able-bodied men.

John's father had grown fond of Egg and Ebenweiler. He loved the beautiful German forests and he wept as the family, carrying their scant belongings, clambered onto the truck that would take them to the train that would take them to yet another resettlement camp where they would face yet another grueling assessment process after which they would finally, finally board a ship bound for the US. (Not everyone could meet the American requirements. The mother of one of John's friends, a woman who had suffered from postpartum depression after giving birth in the camp, killed herself rather than undermine her family's chances at resettlement.)

Jakobīne, Jānis, and their sons left Germany in December 1949.

John was a month and a half shy of his eleventh birthday.

His childhood was over.

40. Oma Learns to Bake Rye Bread (Butler, Pennsylvania, 1950)

What turned Oma (as Jakobīne was known by the time I met her) into a baker of bread was the cellophane-wrapped, presliced knife-in-the-Latvian-heart known as Wonder Bread.

In January 1950, after five years in Germany, John's family, aided by the Lutheran Immigration and Refugee Service and St. Mark's Evangelical Lutheran Church, arrived in Butler, Pennsylvania, a steel mill town in the foothills of the Appalachians. A local business, a tree nursery, gave John's father, a former government agronomist, a job as a laborer and provided the family with a little house that was located seven miles outside of town.

John's family was grateful for the help they received in Butler, but they were confused by the manners, mores, and eating habits of their new neighbors. How could people living surrounded by farmland eat factory-made food without taste, texture, or apparent nutrients?

Their new neighbors found the Melngailis family equally baffling. Take the Sunday after they arrived from Germany.

Jakobīne and Jānis weren't regular churchgoers, but they wanted to say thank you to the congregation for the part they had played in their resettlement. Showing up at St. Mark's in their Sunday best to express their gratitude in person seemed the polite thing to do. Hair slicked down with water, Ivars and John put on their secondhand woolen suits. Jakobīne wore her good silk dress, the one made for her by a Jewish tailor shortly before she married in 1933. Jānis dressed as he did to attend the opera in Riga: morning coat, vest, striped trousers, hat and gloves. Oh yes, and spats. A getup the likes of which had never been seen in Butler, Pennsylvania. Which explains the tittering as the family marched down the center aisle of the church in search of seats on Sunday morning.

The sartorial disconnect was bad enough. The condescension was worse. In the church social hall after the service, balancing cups of weak tea and slices of sheet cake with pink icing served on little paper napkins, the family fielded the same questions again and again. "Didjaever see an indoor terlet?" or "Betjanever used an indoor terlet before." The *terlet* seemed foremost on their new neighbors' minds. In truth, it was the disposable paper napkins—practically new paper, just thrown away!—that caused the Melngailis clan to marvel. (That these awkward newcomers came from a country where a larger percent of the prewar population had earned college degrees than in either France or Germany was utterly beyond the comprehension of their often kind, but startlingly uninformed neighbors.)

Nor could the Butler locals understand why Jakobīne and Jānis allowed eleven-year-old John to barrel down a four-lane highway on his new Schwinn bicycle. The foolhardiness of doing so was the subject of gossip. It seemed beyond the locals' capacity to imagine that John had a job to do: the nearest store was two miles from their house and the family had no other means of transportation.

John rode the Schwinn to the store to buy staples, including that unfathomable American bread. (In his book *Travels in Siberia*, Ian Frazier told a story about the oversized loaves of white bread included in food packages airdropped into Siberia during World War II. Assessing the squishy loaves that fell to the earth, one Russian soldier said that consuming bread like this, a man couldn't squeeze out a respectable shit. This was one Russian sentiment that the Melngailis family heartily endorsed.)

Contemplating a poorly nourished, constipated future for her family, John's mother decided to take matters into her own hands. But where to start when you don't understand the language or the local customs, and wheat, not rye, is the grain grown on surrounding farms? Somehow Oma heard about a farmer growing rye, maybe to feed his pigs, or maybe to make whiskey. She tracked him down and convinced him to sell her a single bushel of unadulterated rye. Another farmer, this one their handsome neighbor who lived across the street, had a small mill that he used to grind corn for pig feed and was willing to help. Using his John Deere tractor as a power source, he ran wheat through the mill to clean out the corn. Then he ran the rye kernels twice through the mill in order to produce rye flour that was neither too coarse nor too fine. As to the sourdough starter? Trained as a pharmacist, Oma understood that bacteria grew wild and could be harvested. She mixed flour and water in a bowl, added warm sour milk, and waited for air bubbles to rise to the surface—these indicated that bacteria were eating, breathing, and reproducing in her bowl. The starter was now a living organism that would stay alive, so long as it was fed and kept in a congenial (not too hot, not too cold) environment. Every other day Oma added warm water and flour to the starter. Soon it smelled just right—pungent and fresh.

Oma's first batches of rye bread were crustless on the outside, and gummy in the center. So soft you could almost eat them with a spoon, which the family did, covered in an eggy custard and topped with jam. (Jakobīne Melngailis did not waste food.)

With practice, her rye bread improved. Her oven was small and not very hot, so she baked her loaves in molds (unheard of in Latvia) and settled for a brownish exterior rather than the fully caramelized brown-black that develops at 500 degrees or more. Still, it lifted her family's spirits to eat rye bread. And providing her family with food that was familiar and nourishing, and that connected them to their roots, lifted her spirits.

In time her rye bread became the talisman of the family's Latvian identity in America. And for John—who changed his name from Jānis when he started high school, finding it unbearable that students denied his maleness, calling him Janice— for John *rupjmaize* became mother and motherland. The past kneaded into the present. Delicious with chunky peanut butter, his favorite American food, then topped with cottage cheese and homemade raspberry jam. Eating such a meal he was at home, heart and soul and body undivided by time and distance and misapprehension.

41. Butler Boyhood

His childhood had gotten waylaid when his family left Germany and moved to the United States. Suddenly the roles were reversed. He and Ivars became the adults. It was they who spoke English. They whom their parents, newly help-less, counted on to navigate the strange new land in which they found themselves. Their school performance, always of great concern, now became the vessel on which the fate of the family would sink or sail. In this regard, John's situation was made worse by his success. At the one-room school he attended during his first two years in Butler, John's skill at math, his quick mastery of English, and his all-around brightness led his teacher to recommend that he skip a grade. Which led to his entering the ninth grade as a physically and emotionally imma-ture thirteen-year-old whose obvious gifts existed side by side with other traits that slowed him down. (In today's argot, John was an intellectually gifted kid with poor executive function who read and processed slowly.) In his own eyes, John was the imperfect younger sibling of an older brother who sailed through school on a cloud of all As, while he was unsure if he was equal to the demands weighing on his boyish shoulders.

42. Alfred Kazin 1

Another anxious, gifted, ambitious son of refugees, the literary critic Alfred Kazin wrote in his memoir *A Walker in the City*, published in 1951, that, regarding his school performance: "I worked on a hairline between triumph and catastrophe." That there were only two possibilities, triumph or catastrophe, was how John felt, too. "It was not for myself alone that I was expected to shine," Kazin wrote, "but for [my parents]." And so it was for John and so many other children of refugees and immigrants, then and now.

43. Old Man

In the summer and on Saturdays, John worked with his father at the tree nursery. It was hard work. Digging up saplings with giant root balls. John sunburned horribly in the summer. And in winter, he froze. But John was young and going places. His father was old and tired. Jānis Senior's feet ached. His back ached. His everything ached. What a life he had stumbled into: at the age of sixty-five, digging holes in the ground.

Soon Ivars would graduate with a bachelor's degree from Carnegie Tech. (Now called Carnegie Mellon University.) Rather than continuing his schooling, John's father decided it was time for Ivars to get a job and support the family so his father could rest.

Oma wasn't having it.

"Old man," she said. "If you don't work, you won't eat."

And that was that. Ivars earned his masters, and then his PhD, in electrical engineering.

44. Suicide 2

Having followed his older brother to Carnegie, John was an overwhelmed, underweight sixteen-and-a-half-year-old freshman the second time he contemplated suicide. He believed (erroneously) that to keep his full scholarship he had to maintain a 3.25 GPA. Math and science, those he could handle. What worried him were the mandatory English and history courses requiring hundreds of pages of reading and writing papers. Adding to his stress, he was living at home, sharing a bedroom with his perfect brother, the graduate student. It was so unfair! John had expected to live in a dorm as an undergraduate, as Ivars had. He graduated from high school as class valedictorian, an achievement that earned him a free ride at Carnegie. Living far out in the country during high school had deprived him of a social life, but finally in college he would be one of the guys. He would live in a dorm. He'd make friends and go to parties. But then his parents decided to follow him to Pittsburgh, where, thanks to their thriftiness, Social Security, and a slice of Ivar's graduate stipend, they were able to buy a house, supporting themselves by taking in boarders. Bye-bye dormitory. Local scholarship kids were required to live at home. So many people under one roof. Brother. Parents. Uncle, whose presence as ersatz family member and paternal best friend was never questioned. Boarders. With just one bathroom. He had no privacy. No friends, no life. As the semester drew to a close, he couldn't sleep. He couldn't think. He couldn't study. He couldn't write papers. Total ruination and humiliation awaited him. There was a railroad bridge in Pittsburgh that Carnegie guys threw themselves off—the school was a pressure cooker. That's what he would do. He would jump off the bridge. What a relief it would be to die. He scoped out the site. He crossed the bridge on foot. Deciding to end his unbearable life calmed him down. A switch in his brain moved from off to on. This had happened to him before: after excruciating terror, amidst oceanic self-hatred, his brain would cohere and he would be saved. He pulled through the semester with perfect grades in math and science and an overall 3.5 GPA. He was safe, but not really safe, because lying ahead, all he could see was three and a half more years of torture.

45. He Survived

As a freshman, he had wanted to study mechanical engineering and join the military reserves. His mother and brother nixed those choices. He skipped the reserves and he majored in physics. Maybe his mother and brother were right or maybe they were not; either way, he did well in physics, better than well, and when he graduated, the physics department recruited him as a graduate student. He won a prestigious graduate work-study fellowship at Westinghouse Research Lab that came with a salary. He published his first paper when he was twenty-one. He dated. He had girlfriends. Lots of girlfriends. None were Latvian, although he was active in Latvian circles. After he passed his PhD qualifying exams he fulfilled a promise to himself, moving out of his parents' house and into his own apartment. (By this time Ivars was living in Boston.) His father accused him of leaving home to pursue sexual immorality. He didn't deny it.

He did not outgrow his mood swings and loopy emotions. He learned to manage them. Sort of. His steady girlfriend when he was in graduate school, a flamboyant art student named Rebecca with a smidge of a drug habit, was herself a bit loopy. They got that about each other. That girlfriend, she also happened to be Jewish.

46. The Price He Paid

John is the only adult I have ever met who remembers every grade he earned in high school, college, and graduate school. He knows his scores on papers and tests, too. His grades weren't recorded in files; they were seared on his flesh.

Inevitably and entirely against his will, he imprinted his children with the need to be perfect and the desperation surrounding this quest.

And one other thing: Living at home during his undergraduate years, it cost him. Connecting with women, that was easy, but all his life, being one of the guys, that capacity, short-circuited in adolescence, eluded him.

47. Primal Journey 3

After he earned his PhD, John spent two years in Europe working as a postdoctoral fellow. These were the most carefree years of his life. He worked, sure, but he also skied and traveled, explored the world, had adventures, ate and drank, and of course, enjoyed many dalliances. The first year, he worked at the Max Planck Institute of Metals Research in Stuttgart. That's where he met Gert and Gerta and other lifelong friends. The second year he worked at Centre national de la recherche scientifique (CNRS) in Paris. Paris! He had bought a white Volkswagen bug when he arrived in Germany. When he moved to Paris, he was required to register the car. When the French bureaucracy informed him that he would have to pay a 20 percent excise tax, he drove halfway across Germany and then on to Switzerland, where he registered the car for a nominal fee, although he didn't live in Switzerland and hadn't bought the car there, either. A coup. Achieved because of his ability to speak languages, his insistence on doing things his own way, his refusal to take no for an answer, and his fondness for racing across Europe in a car.

Patterns of behavior that would last a lifetime were forged.

48. The Ineffable Past

During his two years in Europe, John drove back and forth across Germany numerous times. Once he ventured to Egg hoping to see Heinz. He found his old friend sleeping under a tree. Heinz had become a housepainter and an ardent Jehovah's Witness. The boy with whom John had shared so many adventures had become a man John did not recognize. The past was like that. Ungraspable. Constantly shape-shifting. But John was not deterred. Again and again, he would reach out to grab hold of what was no longer there.

PART THREE

A Rye Bread Marriage

1. Stories in His Head

I thought that people's stories were fixed. John's story? He was a Latvian immigrant who loved rye bread. I thought his passion resembled that of other people who fell in love with a foodstuff that was delicious or healthy or both. If John were not my husband, I might have understood that his connection to Latvian bread was deep and complicated—antediluvian, in fact. I missed this point because I presumed that I knew John inside and out. My self-certainty blinded me. I gazed at a single blossom floating on the pond, and thought I knew the lily pad. I saw the surface, missing the essence: the underwater tangle of roots moving incessantly, connecting acres of blossoms, one to another. Eventually, I realized an entire ecosystem of stories lived inside of John. Each of these stories played a part in forging his identity.

2. Kahlil Gibran

It charmed me when John insisted that we bring an offering of rye bread and salt when visiting friends or family in a new house, but the rest of it, the kissing of a slice of rye bread when it fell on the floor, the ritualized eating a slice with every meal, the scowls that resulted if I left a scrap of rye bread on my plate, the pathological inability to throw out even the tiniest dried-out piece of bread—these habits struck me as excessive. Almost as annoying as his habit of quoting Kahlil Gibran after completing an arduous job. "Work is love made visible," he would tell me after raking leaves in late November when it was cold and damp. Of course, John didn't just rake those leaves, he raked them into a large tarpaulin that he carefully folded as if it were a pastry and then carried to the curb, because John didn't do things the easy way. The idea of shoving leaves into garbage bags offended him. Because, you know, work is love made visible. I found John's devotion to Kahlil Gibran ever so embarrassing. In my view this guy belonged to the refrigerator magnet school of poetry. I preferred *real* poets, like Yeats and Auden.

3. Cultural Memory 1

The conglomeration of stories handed down to each of us from the past has been studied by academics in Germany and elsewhere. They call this form of remembrance Cultural Memory. German scholar Aleida Assmann, author of *Cultural Memory and Western Civilization*, helped develop and popularize the idea of cultural memory as an essential element of individual and group identity. She and her colleagues, including her husband, Jan Assmann, an Egyptologist, theorized that cultural memory was sometimes transmitted through texts or folk art, but more often orally, through stories, myths, religious ritual, and of course, folk song.

4. Cherished Containers

The millions of dainas contain an unparalleled store of Latvian cultural memory. For many Latvians, these short folk songs are not artifacts from a dead or dying past: they are living fonts of meaning, relevant to modern life. I do not speak or read Latvian, but when I began to study translations of dainas related to Latvian history and to rye cultivation, that's when I began to understand the impact of the stories from the past to which John was heir.

5. Stories about Home

Outsiders wonder why Latvians smile so rarely. No doubt the long northern winter has something to do with their downcast expression. Immersing myself in the lyrics of Latvian folksongs, I sensed something else may be at work: A melancholy related to homesickness. A longing for an idealized home that is perpetually out of reach.

Exile is commonplace among John's countrymen. Generation after generation has been driven from their homes due to poverty, war, and exile. Thousands more took to the seas to earn a living because farming was untenable. Many dainas reflect this disruption, suffusing the very idea of *home* with an understated sadness. In these folk songs Latvians long for the beauty of the countryside as they celebrate it.

> Small is my dear home,
> Three gates of copper
> Through one rose the sun,

Through the second, the little moon,
Through the third I drove. Home,
With a yellow little steed.

Other songs about home hint, with the usual Latvian restraint, at the tragic fate that has befallen many Latvian patriots. Such was the case in this four-line poem by the poet Leonīds Breikšs, who was murdered by Stalin in 1942. The first lines illustrated the intimate connection between Latvians and their land.

Nowhere on earth will we be greeted this warmly,
No one will greet us as these fields of grain
Around which reach upward birch tribes
And linden trees look skyward with the wind's voice in them.

According to the geographer E. V. Bunkše, the last two lines of the Breikšs poem were written metaphorically to express the centuries-long Latvian yearning for a homeland. Will this hunger for a homeland ever be sated? Only this can be said with certainty: for many Latvians, *home* and *homesickness* were and often still are one and the same.

6. Stories about Work

Stories from the dainas about work have had a tremendous impact on Latvian identity. In the Latvian imagination, the ancient colonization of Latvia and the theft of Latvian labor by German land barons and the modern colonization of the land by the former Soviet Union have a way of merging.

Historically, some Latvians owned the land they worked, but many did not. They were indentured workers: serfs or slaves, depending on who described their situation. The cruelty inflicted on bonded laborers in Latvia comes close to defying modern comprehension. The Latvian American scholar Maruta Lietiņa Ray identified 1,300 dainas describing the exploitation of Latvian laborers on estates owned by German landlords. "The experience of chronic hunger and extraordinary deprivation became part of the historical memory of Latvian peasants," Ray wrote.

In Ray's view, many Latvian peasants were not serfs with limited legal rights, they were slaves with no rights at all. Call them what you will, for centuries the poorest peasants lived and worked in egregious circumstances on large grain-growing estates owned by absentee landlords. Overseers flogged, tortured, and raped them with impunity. Runaways were punished by having their noses, ears, or even legs amputated. The following daina captures the hopelessness and peculiar self-blame that results from such a life.

> Whither shall I flee, Oh God
> Woods are full of wolves and bears,
> Fields are full of tyrants,
> Punish my father and mother, oh my God,
> Because they raised me in this land of bondage.

German landlords blamed the victims for the ill fortune that befell them. Ugly ideas proclaimed from the pulpit fueled this hatefulness. In the eighteenth century, German preachers condemned Latvians as belonging to one of the nations described in the Old Testament as having been "cursed by God."

7. Identity

If you find it difficult to believe my contention that stories describing the brutality suffered by Latvian serfs generations ago played a part in shaping John's identity and his understanding of the world, I urge you to think again. Think about your own family. I believe all of us, no matter who we are, where we come from, are imprinted by the wounds—and the occasional wonders—of the past. In North America, many believe we arrive on this earth tabula rasa, untouched, our job to create ourselves. I believe such a view is a delusion.

8. Stories about Threshing Rye in Hell and in Heaven

The worst abuses that befell Latvian serfs and laborers were associated with the making of rye bread. These occurred in the threshing houses, where serfs used heavy wooden flails to separate the edible part of the rye from the husk and stalk. Overseers turned these flails on workers who displeased them or failed to give them bribes. To dry the grain (a necessary part of the threshing process), fires burned in threshing houses around the clock. To maximize yield, windows were sealed. Chaff, straw, and dust clogged the hot air. In the dainas, masters' threshing houses are routinely referred to as "hell." Mothers exhorted their sons to do what they could to avoid this work:

Cough and cough continually
You five brothers
Then the lords will think you are old men
And will not send you to the threshing floor.

Another daina, also narrated by a woman, asks why a young worker looks so wan and pale. The answer: "My cheeks are so pale, what has made them so? The master's threshing barn, the acrid smoke, and the dust of the threshing floor."

9. Stories about Stoicism and Resilience

Despite the brutal circumstances in which Latvian workers lived and labored, the formidable Latvian work ethic fortified them. Singing, that most Latvian of activities, sustained their self-respect, fed their resilient spirit, and, upon occasion, justified their arrogance.

Sorrow, sorrow—oh sorrow!
I did not mourn o'er sorrow
I put sorrow 'neath a stone,
Singin walk'd I over it.

10. Cultural Memory 2

From the daina John recited to me long ago urging a Latvian horseman to ride to a far-off land to find a bride, to the Midsummer Festival in New Hampshire that he so loved—what joy for John to lead a ragtag male chorus singing scabrous folk songs mocking women, in response to a female chorus singing songs poking fun at male body parts and male pride—to the memory of the brutal treatment suffered by slaves and serfs on German-owned estates, to the image of that dignified peasant putting his sorrows beneath a stone in his field and singing as he stepped over it, to John's sense of himself as bereft of a home and simultaneously inferior and superior: All these stories lived in John, artifacts of culture and memory handed down for hundreds of years, maybe more.

11. Colliding Stories

Imagine that the stories that have come down to John and me through cultural memory have to do with the value of a man or woman's labor. Though born in the twentieth century to educated parents, an essential part of John's Latvian identity comes from his ability to live up to the dainas teaching that a real man's worth is revealed in his capacity to work efficiently and tirelessly. Hence, the resonance for John of Gibran's line that "work is love made visible." No matter how fatigued he is, regarding work John never complains, and because he does not allow himself to complain, he feels justified in sneering at anyone who does. And say this hard-working man for whom work is love, with roots stretching back to ancient fields of rye, marries a woman like me with different stories in her head. Maybe she is a member of a tribe that was not allowed to own land and that rarely farmed. In her tradition, manual labor is sometimes viewed as a necessary evil. Her grandparents and great grandparents valued study, of course, but working in factories and shops as they did, they also valued protest. Complaint, that least Latvian of activities, was prized by her forebears. (Numerous relatives on both sides of my family were union activists, protesting unfair labor conditions. My maternal grandfather, Meyer Jackins, after whom I am named, was an anarchist.)

In real life John and I are more than the stereotypes attached to our groups. I, for one, like cleanliness and scrubbing, and John is a thinker as well as a worker. Still, our differences regarding labor, manual and otherwise, sometimes set our house on fire. When I complain about shoveling the snow, John cannot help hating me. Because hyperbole is the language of stereotypes, my dislike of shoveling snow might cause him to cast aspersions on my work ethic and the work ethic of my Jewish relatives and friends. Responding to this nonsense, I might add fuel to the rhetorical fire by associating his embrace of anti-Semitic tropes with the fraudulent (and ultimately murderous) *Protocols of the Elders of Zion*—a book proclaiming lies John abhors. The fight, once engaged, can last a long time, moving inevitably toward the bitterly ludicrous. As when my husband expresses the hope—he really did say this—that I will someday be sent to Siberia. He justifies this wish, recalling my refusal to go camping with him after we married despite my prenuptial promise to do so. Camping, he tells me, is about enjoying deprivation, and he believes the punishment for my crimes, named and unnamed, should be deprivation that I am compelled to enjoy. How else will I know what it was like to be a child of war absorbing all his mother's worries, or a teenager required during school vacations to work nine hours a day, six days a week, sometimes in relentless sun and sometimes in bitter cold?

"You hate me for having different stories from you. You hate me because I was born in America in postwar safety, that my summer jobs were cushy, that my parents paid for my college and indulged me in many ways, that I have not grown up afraid in the way you are afraid. It's not my fault," I say. "It is an accident of history."

"No," he answers, "it is your fault."

12. A Third Definition of Marriage

Marriage: A common skin enveloping two individuals, each possessing their own set of vivid stories and memories—personal memories and cultural memories that pertain to the moment in which they were born and to the cultural and political history of their group. Sometimes spouses' stories align like perfectly machined jigsaw puzzle pieces. When that happens, getting along can be easy. When stories clash, however, the bitter arguments that ensue can rip a home apart. Enfolded in these disagreements is the desperate need to preserve the primacy of one's own stories, one's own personal and cultural memories, and by extension, one's own identity. Even when nothing tangible is at stake, it can feel as if everything is at stake.

13. Reading the Text

Sometimes the stories we tell ourselves occlude our vision. Turns out Kahlil Gibran's poem about work has its own meaning, quite removed from John's moralizing or my literary posturing, as is obvious in the poem's last verse:

Work is love made visible.

And if you cannot work with love but only with
distaste, it is better that you should leave your work
and sit at the gate of the temple and take alms of those
who work with joy.

For if you bake bread with indifference, you bake a
bitter bread that feeds but half man's hunger.

And if you grudge the crushing of the grapes, your
grudge distils a poison in the wine.

And if you sing though as angels, and love not the
singing, you muffle man's ears to the voices of the day
and the voices of the night.

—Kahlil Gibran, from The Prophet

And yes, it is utterly amazing that neither John nor I paid
attention to the third line: "If you bake bread with indifference,
you bake bread that feeds but half man's hunger." This line is
the heart of the poem, and it explains everything, about John's
labor and my labor, and how we have managed to stay together
all these years. Neither of us is capable of baking bread with
indifference. In this we are profoundly and indelibly alike.

14. Out of Sequence

I did not know about the power of internalized stories to shape
identity when John and I lived in Newtonville. Only later, after
we had moved to Maryland and John had begun marketing rye
bread and I had started working on this book, did I learn about
cultural memory. Only then, and only gradually, did I open my
mind to the way stories from the past impact identity.

I have placed these chapters here, at the beginning of Part Three, in the hope that they will operate like a three-point light placed by a director to strategically illuminate what comes next.

15.Uprooted

In 1993—when Noah was in the fourth grade, Sarma was at university studying economics, and Ilze, having graduated, was working in Latvia at a women's health clinic—the University of Maryland offered John a full professorship, plus many millions of dollars to set up his own laboratory studying the use of ion beams in the manufacture and repair of microchips. At MIT John's research program thrived, but he relied on soft money; he worried that when his field cooled down, he'd be left underfunded. A full professorship would free him from that rat race—not entirely, but mostly. I didn't want to move. I felt rooted personally and professionally in Boston. I had recently published my second book, a collaboration with a young African American physician who was the health commissioner of Massachusetts, and my sideline, writing for nonprofits, prospered. Still, John's work was steady and he earned significantly more than I did. Since I felt I had no choice, I decided to be strategic about our move. I told John I would move to Maryland if we bought all new furniture, and if we got season tickets to the Kennedy Center.

16. A House Is a Body

Our Newtonville house, the one with the dark woodwork, the oil-guzzling furnace, and the nightmare kitchen, never suited the light freak in me. When we moved to Chevy Chase, we bought a small midcentury modernish brick rambler with many windows, located at the top of a hill. Roll down our street for half a mile and you come to Rock Creek Park, a 1,754-acre urban park with fields and playgrounds and hiking and biking trails that over the years I have come to love almost as much as I love the Massachusetts coast.

17. Farewell

Attending our Page Road goodbye party was like attending my own funeral. Eulogies were delivered. Friends memorialized me as if I were dead. John's and my greatest hits were played and replayed. All those dinners. All those parties.

It's true. In the hosting department, John and I were over the top. Our Boston accountant, when gazing at our tax return one year, had declared that I "was out of control and John was my enabler." In that case, he wasn't even referring to our food costs. He was responding to the money I spent on an evening dress to wear when attending waltz evenings at the Copley Plaza Hotel—ballroom dancing was our new hobby. But yes of course, we hosted dinners before the dances.

Thing is, our farewell party, I didn't want our friends and neighbors to talk about our feats of hospitality. I wanted them to tell me that they loved me.

18. Leaving

Our plan was to pick up Noah at school following our 10 a.m. house closing at the bank, and then drive to Maryland. When we got to Noah's school, a farewell pizza party was in full swing. All the kids from Page Road were crying. Noah was crying. The principal was crying.

If we had set out to make our leave-taking as painful as possible, we couldn't have come up with a better plan.

Noah wept all the way to New Jersey, where we spent the night at a motel with an indoor swimming pool. It didn't help. Neither did fast food and television.

19. Strangers in a Strange Land

Our new neighborhood was not Page Road. Many of our neighbors were older, with grown children. There were some kids on the street, but Noah hadn't known them from birth.

20. Our Nation's Capital

Our new home was in a suburb of Washington, DC. The capital struck me as a weirdly humorless place. Self-serious in the extreme. And lacking in style. My friends in Boston, we all worked, and we all dressed well. Working women in Washington seemed proud *not* to dress well. Moreover, the capital of the free world, our corner of it anyway, was at that time a food desert. There were no Italian or Armenian markets like the ones near our Newton house. No Russo's selling world-class fruits and vegetables, ricotta salata, and soppressata salami, just above wholesale. No fish glistening on beds of ice. The supermarkets near us, Safeway and Giant, were dark and dirty. Shockingly so.

Eventually I heard about Fresh Fields (later bought by Whole Foods), located twenty minutes north of our house. The store was a light-filled oasis. (Or so it seemed at the time.) The abundant

piles of navel oranges and Valencias, mandarins and clemen-
tines, white grapefruit from California, ruby red grapefruit
from Texas, spoke to me of love. And the broccoli, as if picked
yesterday—there were no dirty brown secrets lurking among the
florets, and when I turned the heads upside, as I always do, the
stalks were green and fresh, tip to toe. I burst into tears.

21. Wandering in the Wilderness

John was busy at the university, teaching and setting up his
research program. Noah was busy—I made sure of that. I was
not busy. Not socially and not professionally. I called friends of
friends and asked advice. No one was very helpful: I was told I
should look for government contract work. Writing brochures
for the Small Business Administration. I could imagine nothing
more tiresome. Or humorless.

Bad enough to have no work. Worse not to be known.

22. Cold Calling

Eventually it occurred to me to pick up the phone and cold-call
the development offices at George Washington University and
Georgetown. I described to the people at the other end of the
line the kind of work I had done in Boston. Then I asked if
I could send copies of my clips. Assignments followed. These
assignments kept me busy, and they helped me learn about the
city where I had landed.

23. Carpooling

When we divvied up our children's ethnic identities, we had
agreed that Noah would have a bar mitzvah. In Boston, Noah

had attended Jewish Sunday school at Brandeis, my alma mater. In Washington we joined Temple Sinai, a reform synagogue in the District of Columbia. One of the moms in the Sunday school carpool became my friend. That friendship led to others. In time the feeling of being an outsider waned. Eventually, new acquaintances from Chevy Chase Elementary, Noah's school, and from Temple Sinai started accepting our invitations.

24. Going Without

We tried ordering rye bread from Hartford when we moved to Chevy Chase, but it never really worked. The bread arrived late and in poor condition. Soon the Hartford baker went out of business.

It seemed to me that John barely noticed. His job at Maryland challenged him in new ways. Teaching courses, which he'd never done on a regular basis, took up a lot of energy. Committee assignments kept him busy, too—he'd been more or less exempt from these in the past, and of course, he had a research program to build. I don't know if he thought about rye bread, but he didn't talk about it with me. He did talk about missing the Latvian community in Boston, but he did little to connect with Latvians living in Maryland and DC. Community events were centered at the Latvian Lutheran Church that he would not join.

The human heart: Is there anything more perverse?

25. Rebecca at the Well (November 1996)

Noah's bar mitzvah was a shindig to remember. One hundred and forty people, family and friends from every phase of our lives, most especially our neighbors from Page Road, along with Ilze and Sarma—both living and working in New York, Ilze at Planned Parenthood, Sarma at Bear Stearns—and my wheelchair-bound, ninety-seven-year-old grandmother, who had traveled with her aide and my mother.

The bar mitzvah was about Noah, still skinny and small, still a boy, but a boy poised on a precipice. In my view, it was also a moment to declare á la Elaine Stritch and Stephen Sondheim, "I'm still here!" I had survived our move. We had survived our move. We had made a new life and now we were partying.

Noah interpreted his Torah portion, Rebecca at the Well, as a celebration of hospitality. Neither of us can remember if this was his idea or mine, but I think it was his. I remember being surprised that he thought about such things. I was pro–bar mitzvah, but I had my doubts about thirteen-year-old boys interpreting scripture. John did not. Having been a skinny, unsure boy himself, John thought it a beautiful, spirit-bolstering custom to shower a half-cooked thirteen-year-old with attention. Speaking to his son on the bimah (as is the reform practice), John expressed his wish that Noah would become the kind of man who can admit when he is wrong. A man cannot do science or anything worthwhile, John said, unless he is able to review his own actions and admit his mistakes.

26. Milestone

Shortly after the bar mitzvah, I turned fifty.

I embraced my marriage, I loved being a mom and a stepmom, I adored my friends, but I was not satisfied with myself.

I had watched my father flounder in his late mid-life, unable to actualize himself or accept his own shortcomings. I was determined to unstick myself. The way I saw it, my fifties posed a developmental challenge. Either I would grow as a person and as a writer in the coming decade or, metaphorically speaking, I would collapse and begin to die.

In Boston I had seen three or four therapists, none for very long. One had told me I couldn't be depressed because I looked too good. (I had arrived at her office dressed for meeting.) Her superficiality stunned me. When a close friend in New York went into psychoanalysis, that least superficial form of therapy, I decided to try psychoanalysis, too.

27. Dr. L

Dr. Lowey was a male psychoanalyst, nearly seventy, with a sweet face. Like John, he was a multilingual World War II refugee. I loved being in Dr. Lowey's presence, although for the first two years of our relationship I didn't let him get a word in edgewise.

I saw Dr. Lowey once or twice a week, on and off for eight years. The last two years, I graduated myself from the couch to a chair.

This therapy was either a huge success or a terrible failure. Or both. Dr. Lowey was not a feminist. In that sense, I am not sure he fully understood my struggles. But he was deep. And the opposite of facile. He saw things that I did not see. (Which is why I tried so hard to talk over him.) He taught me that my self-hating rants were self-protective. "Self-soothing," to use his language. He taught me to do nothing until I knew what I wanted to do. Most especially, he taught me to shut up long enough to hear myself think.

28. Adult Bat Mitzvah

I enrolled in an adult bat mitzvah class at Temple Sinai.

I wanted to find out if I was a religious person.

29. Pain in the Ass

A friend of a friend had introduced John and me to a couple who had moved to Chevy Chase around the time we did. Mark and Elise were academics with an only child who was grown. Our lives quickly became entwined. Mark, the husband, was a psychology professor; he and John played racquetball together. Elise was a medical doctor and researcher. She knew a lot about healthcare, and she became a valued journalistic source. But there was a dark side to our friendship. Elise and Mark were triangulators who tried to drive a wedge between John and me. Like a pair of Iagos, they whispered in my ear about John's shortcomings. They said he took me for granted. They pointed out his lapses in consideration, his refusal to listen when I asked him when pulling out of our drive to *pleeeeeeassse* slow down while I fastened my seat belt. They were offended by John's stories extolling the virtues of other women, especially his first wife.

The subtext of Mark and Elise's critique: that I was more evolved than John and perhaps I would be better off without him. Never mind the fact that John loved me, that he was devoted to our family, and that he championed and financially supported my writing career. (Never mind that his misbehavior was often triggered by his sensing disapproval, especially female disapproval.) Mark and Elise's assessment of John tickled my vanity and at first their campaign made headway. John traveled for work, and when he was away the three of us went to the movies on Saturday nights and afterward, we would sit near one another on the living room couch drinking red wine and dissecting John's psyche. The upshot of our conversations: John was a pain in the ass.

Then one morning on the phone, Elise revealed more than she intended: she told me she knew she must tread lightly regarding her critique of John's character because in the past, after criticizing their husbands, she had lost two women friends.

Ms. Iago gave away her game.

Contemplating her words, I realized I had been pulled off course by a woman with a track record of marital meddling whose own marriage was wobbly at best. In the aftermath of this incident, I thought about the odd and yet necessary insularity of marital relationships. I realized my folly in letting untrustworthy outsiders worm their way beneath the epidermis protecting the inner workings of John's and my marriage.

Yes, some of John's habitual behaviors annoyed me. And, yes, sometimes he was downright obnoxious, especially when he smelled female disapproval. But what about me? Was I really such a paragon? Did I not, when frustrated, stand with my hands on my hips delivering broadsides enumerating my mate's shortcomings? Could it be that I annoyed and frustrated John as he much as he did me? Could it be that John was not the only pain in the ass in our marriage?

30. Other People Are Real

Something fundamental in my thinking shifted when I understood that I, too, was a pain in the ass and that my point of view was only one point of view. I still found John's behavior hard to tolerate at times, that didn't change, and we certainly did not stop bickering, nor, in general, did my behavior improve, but I could see that my husband did not exist to be a moon to my sun. He was not an object in relation to a subject. He was a person with his own thoughts, with his own secrets, his own stories, who was as real to himself as I was real to me. That was the important part: *That he was as real to himself as I was to me.*

And so, a few years past fifty, I discovered what I believe: Other people are real.

That is my morality.

That this four-word sentence is an amalgam of Jewish and psychoanalytic thinking about *the other* did not occur to me at the time, but, of course, it is.

31. When You Know You Are Really Married

As married as I was—and I was very married—a tiny part of my reptile brain remained on the lookout for the perfect man. You know, the fairytale husband I was supposed to be with, a man who did not fetishize rye bread or constantly assert his foreignness. A man who read the same books as I, who adored wit and banter as much as I did—as opposed to John, who said, "Just because you are eloquent doesn't mean you are right." Then in 1999, two months before his sixtieth birthday, when we had been living in Maryland for six years, John was diagnosed with prostate cancer. A certain part of me was not surprised by his diagnosis. John was so invested in his masculinity—and so pleased with himself in that department. And fate is such a nasty bitch. As we sat in the doctor's office clutching each other's hands, the frat-boy urologist on the other side of the desk told us there was nothing to worry about. Nothing! Because if the surgery happened to go bust—"No worries!" He could do a penile implant! Fifteen minutes after meeting us, one week after John's diagnosis, he really said that. Cinderella time ended just like that. John's cancer revealed the simple truth that I was living my real life. John and I were married for the long haul. One of us would bury the other.

32. A New Definition of Marriage

Marriage: Two people who have tasted mortality. Two people walking hand and hand into the sunset.

33. Radiation

Elise, the would-be marriage assassin, had stayed in our life. Nominally, we were still friends, although I no longer trusted her. Elise had contacts at the National Institute of Health and arranged for John to talk to the director of the National Cancer Institute about radiation as opposed to surgery to treat prostate cancer. The data on surgery versus radiation at his age and level of illness was inconclusive. The NCI guy recommended that John talk to the head of radiation at Georgetown Lombardi Comprehensive Cancer Center. Being irradiated didn't scare John. He understood how radiation worked, and after thinking it over, he decided he preferred it to surgery. In fact, he had two forms of radiation, one experimental. The treatment was no piece of cake.

Hemingway said courage is grace under pressure. That was John during his treatment and aftermath. Grace under pressure. Stoic but not stuffy. With his sense of humor intact. Before commencing treatment, he took a drug that temporarily reduced his ability to produce testosterone. (Authorities use this drug to chemically castrate men convicted of sex crimes.) Sarma asked if the lack of testosterone meant he stood in front of his closet every morning wringing his hands, bemoaning the fact that he had nothing to wear.

He thought her joke was a riot.

34. The Emotional Container

John's diagnosis terrified me. I carried the emotion for us both. I was terrified that our life would change. That our relationship would change. I couldn't imagine who we would be, who I would be, without the sexual energy moving back and forth between us. I wasn't primarily worried about sex as a verb, although I was worried about that, too; what frightened me was the possibility that John's essence as a human would change, altering the connection between us.

The drug made John (temporarily) impotent, but it didn't

change him that much. He still drove with his dick. Shut down his testosterone supply and John was still John.

But my fear lived on.

35. The Pig

John's treatment extended over four and a half months, culminating in early June 2000 when he spent a week more or less upside down in Georgetown Hospital being intermittently irradiated by a machine called a pig. (That's a medical term describing a lead container for shipping or storing radioactive materials. Its thick walls protect medical staff while treating patients.)

36. Racing Across Europe in a Volvo

That summer we had complicated travel plans. The Georgetown medical team had assured us John would be A-OK to travel. (Life lesson: never trust medical specialists when they tell you this stuff. They don't have a clue about normal recovery.) Two days after John left the hospital, after undergoing a week of weirdly invasive experimental treatments, we flew to St. Petersburg with Noah, who was seventeen and studying Russian. We toured that city, then took a train to Riga, where we visited family. From Riga we took a ferry to Stockholm, where we picked up John's new Volvo. We raced across Denmark to northern Germany, dropped Noah off at the airport at Hamburg (he had a job in New Hampshire in August working as a counselor at his beloved summer camp). Then John and I crossed France and Belgium in the new car that we later shipped home for free, which you could do in those days. (The manufacturer picked up the cost.) During most of the trip John was uncomfortable and exhausted. Touring Autun, a Roman site in Burgundy, he lay down on a sun-warmed stone wall, groaned, and said all he wanted to do was go to a beach and lie in the sun. We'd been married for nearly eighteen years, and I had never heard John complain in that way. In Brussels on our last night, John and I argued about where to eat dinner. The fight wasn't pretty. I stood in Brussels's historic Grand-Place detailing my grievances with John's character, his controlling insistence that he make all of our travel decisions, his habit of racing across Europe in a car, and his weirdness with money, veering from one moment to the next between cheapness and profligacy. It was our last night abroad and it was my God-given right to eat our one dinner in Brussels at a bistro recommended by the guidebook. Not a great place. Just a good place with good food. And this went on until neither of us had an appetite. And it didn't matter that some of what I said was true, because my obliviousness to John's suffering was inexcusably cruel.

Dear Reader: Beware the narrator who seeks to portray herself in the best light. Who charms you with her kindness and empathy. Because in moldy corners of her being, she is just as primitive and self-obsessed and rageful as everybody else. Maybe more so.

37. The Limitations of Memory 1

John insists now that our argument in Brussels concerned where to stay that night, not where to eat. He might be right. Until

Airbnb arrived on the scene, and I became the family online booker, we often argued about hotels. John favored fleabags: ratty digs comforted him, as odd as that may sound. Regarding restaurants, his standards tended to be higher. Still, I'm sticking with my story. When you write a memoir, you take possession of memories that belonged to both of you—sometimes even memories belonging to him alone—and you make them yours.

38. The Limitations of Memory 2

Having read this book several times, John sometimes uses my language and details that I unearthed when telling his story. He has no idea that input from me has altered his memory.

39. Radiation Worked

John has been cancer-free for more than twenty years.

40. New Directions (2002)

I was looking for something. A place to land.

Dr. Lowey suggested that I enroll in a Washington-based writing program for scholars and therapists interested in psychoanalysis. It was called New Directions. I was neither a scholar nor a therapist, but I decided to apply, and I was accepted.

I found many new friends and an intellectual home at New Directions. Also, almost by accident, I found a new direction for my writing.

I decided that my next book would be a psychologically informed exploration of some aspect of ordinary life. My first idea, to write a users' guide to psychotherapy, did not pan out. My thoughts turned next to food. I wrote a proposal for a book I called *Love and Hate in the Kitchen*. My agent at the time sent this proposal out and it came close to selling. But it didn't sell. Publishers were leery because I was neither a therapist nor a food writer. Well, I said: I can write about food.

41. Food Writer (2004)

The Washington Post food section had a new editor, and she was looking for freelancers. She liked my quirky ideas. Soon I was writing food articles for the *Washington Post*.

42. The Geopolitics of Rye Bread

After the collapse of the former Soviet Union, Latvian Americans were free to travel to Latvia, and many, including John and his brother, did just that. (Ivars's American-born son, a banker, married a Latvian woman, and settled there.) Bureaucratically speaking, Latvia was a bit of a mess—throughout the 1990s, the streets of Riga thronged with Russian gangsters. Still, returning to a free, incipiently democratic Latvia meant a tremendous amount to Latvian Americans. And post-Soviet Latvia was showing itself to be a lively and questing place. As capitalism geared up there, dozens of would-be entrepreneurs interested in marketing products that were native to their country began baking and selling bread in Riga's Central Market and elsewhere. Returning home to the US, travelers, including John, filled empty suitcases with *rupjmaize* and other delicious rye breads—so long as the bread was cellophane-wrapped, it could be brought into the US, though, yes, drug-sniffing dogs did take notice.

In 2004 everything changed. Latvia joined the European Union. Suddenly it was easy to airfreight rye bread from Latvia to the US.

In 2006, John began ordering *rupjmaize* for our personal consumption baked by Riga's famed *Lāči* bakery.

43. Black Rooster Food 1

My work for the *Washington Post* had me out and about, attending events and meeting local food people, some of whom became my friends, our friends. When John and I served Latvian rye bread with smoked salmon to our new buddies, they went wild. Their enthusiasm encouraged John to join forces with his racquetball partner Ken, a chemist born in Egypt who taught an entrepreneurship class at the University of Maryland business school. The two of them formed an LLC and they began air-freighting rye bread from Riga to Washington that they sold to Whole Foods. They called their company Black Rooster Food—Melngailis, John's last name, means "black rooster."

44. Black Rooster Food 2

Every other week John left his office at the University of Maryland in College Park late Thursday afternoon, facing the infamous traffic on Interstate 495, on his way to Dulles Airport in Virginia. At the airport he handed over his paperwork and backed an oversized rental truck into the receiving area, where he retrieved pallets of rye bread in hundred-pound boxes taped together by the export company in Riga. John cut the pallets apart and repackaged the bread by hand for delivery to his customers. The huge truck was necessary to negotiate the loading dock at the Whole Foods warehouse in Landover, Maryland—most of the bread was destined for Whole Foods. After completing his work at Dulles, John drove the huge truck to our house, left it on the street overnight, drove to the Whole Foods warehouse at six the next morning, returned the truck to the rental company, retrieved his car and drove to the university to begin his day. He was sixty-seven years old.

Then the value of the euro in relation to the dollar skyrocketed, causing the price of jet fuel to rise precipitously. Shipping costs went through the roof, and importing bread from Latvia became unsustainable. That was the end of Phase One of Black Rooster Food.

45. Black Rooster Food 3

John is not a man to give up.

He went looking for a baker in New York (where many potential customers were located) who could bake *rupjmaize*. After calling around, he found a Belarusian immigrant named Gennadiy Verebeychik who owned a successful bakery in Coney Island called New York Bread. John asked Gennadiy if he was interested in baking Latvian-style rye bread. Gennadiy had never baked rye bread without some percentage of wheat flour, but he was willing to try. John gave him samples of rye breads baked in Latvia. It took a number of attempts, but pretty soon Gennadiy's baker had mastered the craft and New York

Bread began turning out Latvian rye, which John marketed to upscale stores up and down the East Coast, from Boston to Maryland.

46. Coffee

In the early days of Black Rooster Food, I was often out of town traveling for work. In 2005 I had written a story for the *Post* about the upscaling of office coffee. Reporting that piece, I realized that specialty coffee was big, and it was going to get bigger. I decided to jump on that train. On my own dime—on our own dime—I traveled to Latin America to meet coffee growers and attend coffee competitions. I wrote a story about specialty coffee in Panama and Nicaragua, published by the *New York Times,* that helped establish me as someone in the know. I wrote other stories about coffee. Later I journeyed to East Africa with three young coffee buyers and wrote a book about my adventures that provided readers with a bird's-eye view of the high-end coffee business.

47. A Man with a Cause

Looking youthful in jeans and a Brooks Brothers shirt, brimming with belief in his product, John would walk into a specialty store and begin to talk about rye bread with the bread manager or whoever would listen. If he found a receptive audience, he would take a quarter loaf of bread from his backpack, cut a piece with his own knife, and hand it over. Usually a conversation would ensue, during which John would talk about his mother baking rye bread when his family came to America.

When asked a more practical question about the bread's shelf life, John would reach into his backpack, take out another chunk of bread, this one baked five weeks earlier, and cut a slice, proving his bread was virtually indestructible. With age, the bread lost some of its moisture, and the flavors evolved, but the bread stayed tasty and intact, the long shelf life a boon to storekeepers and consumers alike.

John's conviction and the quality of his product proved to be a winning formula. Gourmet stores in New York, Washington, DC, and Boston took him on as a vendor. Scott Goldshine, general manager of Zabar's; Niki Russ Federman, the fourth generation co-owner of Russ & Daughters; chef Marcus Samuelsson (who later served Black Rooster rye with homemade gravlax at his restaurant Red Rooster Harlem); Ruth Reichl, former editor of *Gourmet magazine*; food writer Michael Pollan; and an endless number of other food writers and bloggers became fans.

Not that John was content selling rye to famous writers and foodies. He had a bigger dream: changing the American diet, replacing processed white bread with heart-healthy, fiber-rich rye, thereby reducing the incidence in the US of obesity, diabetes, and some cancers, not to mention alienation, depression, and crooked teeth. I found John's enthusiasm over the top, but his belief in rye bread had merit: rye grain had long been recognized for its superior nutritional profile and high fiber content. Now investigators in the US, Scandinavia, and elsewhere were publishing papers proclaiming the healthfulness of fermented foods such as rye bread, yogurt, tofu, kombucha, and sour pickles, in which specific species of living bacteria had been encouraged to grow. John saw himself as a spokesman for a movement. At every store he visited, he banged the drum for healthy eating. "I've bought myself a soapbox," he'd say.

48. Latvian Schlepping Gene

I marveled at John's willingness to tolerate the discomfort of schlepping boxes and bundles, valises and backpacks, cold packs and display tables, from one destination to another.

At least once a month he drove 225 miles north from our house in Maryland to the bakery in Brooklyn, where he loaded his car with cases of bread for sampling. From Brooklyn he drove to upscale markets in New York City, New Jersey, Westchester, and Long Island, contending with the traffic, the byzantine parking rules, the indigenous bad manners, and the weight and awkwardness of carrying his display table, brief-case, and overstuffed refrigerated backpack. At each destina-tion, he spent hours and hours and hours standing on his feet while talking, talking, talking about his favorite subject. He did this several days in a row and then returned to his job at the University of Maryland (where he had cut back to half time).

49. His Roots

In marketing Latvian rye bread, John found a meaningful way to reconnect with his Latvian roots while contributing to the Latvian community. He did all this without joining the local Latvian church, although he did attend concerts and other events there, where he enjoyed long conversations with the

pastor, a woman whom he deemed to be exceptionally intelligent and *sympatique*. We began attending events hosted by
the Latvian ambassador and his wife at the Latvian Embassy
on Massachusetts Avenue, which often served Black Rooster
bread.

50. His Mission

When John was convinced of the rightness of a mission, he had
a talent for convincing others. He was what academics call a
transformative leader. He saw things that others did not see;
and he possessed a kind of reasoned conviction, combined with
passion, that attracted others to his cause. An ants-in-the-pants
kind of guy, he enjoyed being out and about. He enjoyed selling. He did not enjoy the more mundane aspects of leadership.
He stank as an administrator.

51. Sweet Butter

John and I sent a five-pound loaf of *rupjmaize* to my friend and
editor Jeff Bailey, in Chicago. His thank-you note blew my socks
off. Jeff was a business writer—I freelanced for him at the *Wall
Street Journal* and *Crain's Chicago Business*—but something
in John's bread brought out his inner Anthony Bourdain. Jeff
told us that until he tasted Latvian rye with sweet butter, "I
didn't know what sweet butter was for." It never occurred to
him, he wrote, "that two foods, lean and fat, sour and *umami*,
hard and soft, smooth and pebble-y, could be so well suited as
to define one another. Rye bread and sweet butter give each
other a reason to exist."

52. Title Without a Book

After the coffee book was published, I knew I wanted to write another book, another narrative. I woke up one morning in early 2010 and told John that the title of my next book would be *The Rye Bread Marriage*. The title arose unbidden—at the time I had written not one word about rye bread. I recognized immediately that a book with this title would allow me to tell John's family story—I had long been eager to do that. Furthermore, it would allow me to explore the idea that had recently suggested itself to me, that rye bread connected John's family story and mine. I had a hunch, based on geography, that the rye bread my grandmother Hannah ate in Slutsk, the shtetl in the Belarusian province of Minsk where she was born, closely resembled Latvian *rupjmaize*. That it would take ten years for me to figure how to tell this story, I had no idea, and that was probably a good thing.

53. Pitchman

Sometimes, like John, I did stints passing out bread samples in the Whole Foods near our home—that was fun. But the best was Zabar's, New York's beloved "deli" located on Broadway and West 80th Street. Zabar's and I went back. I had shopped there during the thirteen years I lived on the Upper West Side.

54. Zabar's

I was handing out tiny triangles of *rupjmaize* at Zabar's on a sunny Saturday in October 2010. Not for the faint of heart: Zabar's on Saturday afternoon. A propulsive flow of energy pushed a swarm of food foragers through a maze of aisles, past racks and display counters. Square footage—square inch-age, really—counts for everything at Zabar's. Which explains why I was squashed in front of a refrigerated display case adjacent to a heavy swinging door through which a sweet-faced Dominican man periodically exited, shouting, "Coming through. Coming through," as he grazed my display table with his overloaded cart. Still, my perch was prime. To cross from one side of the store to the other, customers had to pass directly in front of my little table.

"Care to taste a traditional sourdough rye bread?" I asked again and again. "It's an Old World recipe. Hand-made containing one hundred percent whole-grain rye flour." Some shoppers seized pieces of bread on the fly, like marathoners grabbing cups of water from outstretched hands. Others slowed to a full stop before reaching for a sample and popping it in their mouths. Maybe one in ten shoppers picked up a package of bread from the display rack and peered at the label. Often, they dropped the package into their basket. Sometimes they did not.

"Our bread fights back when you bite into it," I said with a practiced laugh. "And nothing is more nutritious than rye."

"I buy this bread every week," one woman said, dismissing my sales pitch. "I know about good bread. I used to own a bakery. We baked rye bread." I struggled to place her accent. German? Russian? As we chatted she dropped one, two, and then three quarter-loaves of our neatly packaged bread into her basket. Turns out she was Israeli.

"Where was your bakery?" I asked. "In Tel Aviv?"

"No. It was in Queens," she said. "Queens, New York. But I learned about rye bread in Israel. My grandmother escaped from Poland and settled in Herzliya, north of Tel Aviv. She owned a beauty shop where I went after school. Next door was a bread bakery. The smell of fresh-baked rye bread filled my grandmother's shop. When I think about my grandmother, that's what I remember. The fragrance of rye bread."

"This is the healthiest bread in the world," said a blondish woman with flyaway hair as she joined us, picking up a package of bread and peering at the label. She admired the logo, recently redesigned by our future son-in-law, before tossing the loaf into her basket.

The two women stood at my table extolling the virtues of rye bread. Its nutritional superiority. Its three-week shelf life. Its high fiber content.

I said nothing. Why should I, when these customers were doing my job? When the conversation turned to breakfast, I joined in, forming a culinary chorus. In the morning we three liked our rye bread:

Sliced thin and topped with peanut butter and black
    currant jam
Dripping with raw honey and almond butter
Bubbling with melted goat cheese and topped with fig
    jam
Sopping up the yolk of an soft-boiled organic egg
Soaking up the fat from thick slices of bacon.

(One delicious combination was missing from our contra-puntal conversation: smashed avocado on top of rye bread. In 2010, we had not yet visited San Francisco and discovered the wonders of avocado toast. Shortly after that trip, John began touting what he called rye bread crostini: honey mustard, smashed avocado, sliced radish, and sea salt on rye bread.)

A small group gathered around us. Food talk, like food writing, provides its own form of sustenance.

The bits of bread on my tray disappeared quickly. Using a carbon steel chef's knife from our home kitchen—a serrated bread knife is pretty useless when slicing through the tough crust and solid interior of a five-pound loaf—I carved a dozen more slices, subdividing them into many small triangles, each with a bit of crust. (To judge the excellence of any bread, your teeth need to make contact with both the crust and the crumb—that's the bakers' term for the interior of the bread.)

"I hate rye bread," a chunky woman in a red sweater said defiantly as she scurried past me to the pastry section.

A young guy carrying a bike helmet picked up a quarter loaf, peering at the label. He told me he bakes bread. "Rye flour is miserable to work with . . ."

"Which is why most rye bread contains wheat flour," I answered, adding that this bread was different. "It has no wheat."

"No wheat? Does that mean your bread is gluten free?" asked a super-slender woman with one of those cheek-sucking, characterologically unhappy faces I associate with Beverly Hills and the Upper East Side of Manhattan.

"Rye has less gluten than wheat bread, but it is not gluten free," I answered.

She picked up a loaf, looked carefully at the label, and then returned it, with a small shudder, to the display rack. "I never eat bread," she said, her tone reminding me of a guest at a long-ago dinner party who turned her wine glass upside down on the table when a simple "no thanks" would have delivered the message.

I sighed, knowing they came in waves, these legions of bread-haters.

"This bread has salt," chimed in a well-dressed guy in his thirties, his voice accusatory.

"All bread has salt," I answered. "Flour. Water. Salt." (In fact, all bread does not contain salt: Tuscan bakers put no salt in their white bread, and I later learned from the bread historian William Rubel about a village in a mountainous region of France that famously baked loaves of hearty rye in the fall that contained no salt and that lasted them an entire winter. But I didn't know any of that at the time.)

"This bread has too much salt," Mr. High Class Haberdashery replied.

I surreptitiously checked my watch.

"This here is pumpernickel bread," stated an older guy in a blue fleece and running shoes.

"Pumpernickel means a lot of things to a lot of people," I said.

"Girlie, this here is pumpernickel bread," he repeated emphatically, pointing to loaves of Black Rooster Baltic Rye stacked on the display table next to me as he walked away. (According to baker and scholar Stanley Ginsberg, pumpernickel is a coarse, almost crust-less rye bread from Westphalia, Germany, that is baked in a form and is steamed for twenty-four hours in a cool oven. I offer this information advisedly: traditional foods such as pumpernickel don't stop evolving when they reach a classic form. Traditional foods evolve and keep evolving.)

"Can I take another piece?" asked a tall young woman. "My grandmother was born in Sweden and she baked bread like this."

"Latvia and Sweden are neighbors on the Baltic," I said. "Their breads are similar. Not surprising your grandma's bread tastes like *rupjmaize*."

A middle-aged man in a tweed jacket standing off to the side looked at me knowingly and said, "But you are not Latvian, are you?" Inwardly I sighed. I knew what came next.

"My husband is Latvian," I said. "And two of my grandparents were Russian Jews who identified as Litvaks." (The term *Litvak* refers to Jews who lived in a large area of Eastern Europe whose borders kept changing but that included parts of Latvia, Poland, Belarus, Prussia and Lithuania.) "His ancestors and mine lived within a few hundred miles of each other and they all ate a lot of rye bread. You might say rye bread ties our 'mixed marriage' together," I said expansively.

He didn't buy my spiel. "I can't see that Jews and Latvians have much in common," he said without a trace of a smile. It pained me, this assumption of enmity.

"History weighs on us all," I said, and turned my attention to cutting more bread. There was a pause in the flow of customers. Then a chap in a belted brown leather coat approached.

"May I?" he asked, as he picked a bit of bread off my little white tray. He paused. "This bread is delicious," he said.

"It goes well with the smoked salmon in your basket," I said. "It also goes with herring," I added.

I had said the magic word.

"Herring!" he said. "Herring! I love herring. Just hearing the word takes me back to my Bubbe's kitchen."

"At our house we serve rye bread with herring and tiny shot glasses filled with ice-cold vodka."

"Oh my God," he said, sounding like a guy who'd just discovered sex. (Amazing, really, the passion of affluent New Yorkers for what John lovingly calls "peasant food," by which he means delicious, simple foods eaten by poor people in traditional societies.)

As I packed up and prepared to depart, a handsome fellow in a blazer, with Finno-Ugric eyes, swung by my display table and took a sample of bread.

"I know this bread. I grew up on this bread," he said. He closed his eyes and took another bite, letting the firm tidbit melt in his mouth. A smile crossed his face and traveled to his now open eyes. His face relaxed. I recognized his Proustian expression. He did not like this bread. He loved this bread. The bread of memory. The bread of the lost motherland. The lost mother.

"Can I really buy this bread here?" he asked.

"Yes, you can."

"Every week? Really?"

"Yes," I said. "You can by this bread every week."

And then he leaned over and kissed the lapel of my purple corduroy blazer. This was not a flirtatious gesture.

"Thank you," he said. "I love this bread."

"I do, too." I said; and as I spoke I realized that something had shifted inside me. I said it again, just to hear myself say the words. "I love this bread."

55. Our Family Brand

We ate Black Rooster bread in the morning and talked about marketing rye bread at night. When our friends visited, we served smoked salmon on rye bread. For the first time in our married life, our professional worlds overlapped: I was a food writer with an interest in history and culture, and John marketed a gourmet product with roots in Eastern Europe.

Rye bread was our signature. We shipped loaves of *rupjmaize* to friends and family all over the country, helping them celebrate holidays and happy occasions and find comfort when they were sad. Sometimes we shipped bread to friends for no reason at all.

56. Latvia (2010)

The summer before that visit to Zabar's, John and I had spent a month in Latvia so I could begin to learn about rye bread and its history. John had visited Latvia several times without me, but the two of us had not been there together since 2005.

In 2010 I insisted on planning the trip *my* way. There would be no racing across the vast expanse of the European continent in a car, and we weren't going to stay in a dump. Moreover, we would remain in one place long enough for me to feel truly present. Happily, John's brother now owned a beautifully renovated apartment in Riga's historic art deco district where we could stay for free.

57. Lielvārde

We were in our little white rental, heading east out of Riga toward Lielvārde to meet John's friend Aivars Grinbergs, a rye bread baker and builder of bread ovens.

It took half an hour to traverse Riga's labyrinth of streets, rattle across the neglected cobblestone railroad bridge, and escape onto a modern highway, courtesy of the European Union. As cityscape gave way to rural vista, we glimpsed an unattractive concrete hydroelectric dam that spanned the Daugava River at its broadest point—upgraded by the Russians with the usual Soviet disregard for quality materials and design. The road turned away from the river, and we found ourselves driving through field after field of low-growing, yellow-flowering rapeseed, the stuff from which canola oil is made. The furrows were regular and deep—the earth, leased by Scandinavian agricultural multinationals as was much Latvian farmland, had been laid open by giant machines, equipment that local farmers could not afford. Some skeptical Latvians considered the wholesale leasing of Latvian farmland to outsiders, along with the raft of regulatory practices instituted by the EU, as proof that Europe and Scandinavia were bureaucratic interlopers rigging the rules for their own benefit, not all that different, in this view, from the former Soviet Union.

John interrupted my musings. "That sign we just passed said A6. I thought we were supposed to be on E22."

I peered into the map on my lap. (In 2010, GPS in Latvia was still pretty useless.) "A6 and E22 are the same road," I said.

"You need to pay attention. I don't want to get lost," John said.

"Stay on the A6/E22. It goes south past Lielvārde all the way to Lithuania," I answered.

"In the other direction, it goes straight to Moscow," John said. "I looked at the map before we left."

"You looked at the map?"

"I didn't want to get lost," John said.

"If you looked at the map, why are you hectoring me?"

"I drive. Following our route on the map is your job," he answered.

I was going to say something nasty, but then I looked over and saw John was oozing nervous energy. He looked like a Labrador on a leash straining to sink his teeth into a T-bone. If he could have bounced his leg up and down while driving a manual transmission, he'd have been doing it. John had been born in Lielvārde. He lived there during his first five years. Even though he had visited before, going home was weighted with emotion that John seemed unable to acknowledge or process. And so, I was left to intuit what John was thinking and feeling while he cast aspersions on my map-reading skills. Which I did, and he did, again and again, leading me to think of this form of interplay as a marital version of what psychoanalysts refer to as the repetition compulsion.

We arrived half an hour early.

John parked the car and we walked over to the railroad station, where a woman and small child sat on a bench in the morning sunshine waiting for the train to Riga. At her side: a basket covered with a linen towel containing what? Strawberries from her garden? Pirogues? Homemade *rupjmaize* for her Riga relatives?

John's family house was located three hundred feet from the station. There was a flower shop in the first-floor storefront where, seventy-five years earlier, the pharmacy, with its wooden floor, hand-operated cash register, and multiple rows of glass jars full of pharmaceutical chemicals and compounds, had flourished. The rest of the first floor housed a children's art school. In what had been the garden, a freestanding cafeteria in front of which many trucks were parked.

58. The Man Who Loved Rye Bread

Aivars was waiting for us outside his house. He and John greeted each other with affectionate restraint. Half hugs. Claps on the back. Aivars's looks were ordinary. Medium height. Bald head. Glasses. Then he smiled an impish smile and I got it. He was a charmer. I would have guessed his age as early fifties, but he was ten years older.

We followed Aivars through his garden, stopping to admire the beds of tall white daisies, dill weed, parsley, and onions thrusting out of the earth, alongside a bramble of berry bushes and a small orchard of pruned and gnarly apple and pear trees. Bird feeders hung from fruit trees. Two small chairs under an apple tree made me think of a forest glade. Someplace magical. Aivars pointed to a pair of small swallowlike birds diving gracefully into the tall grass of the un-mown field on the edge of the property. The birds had made their nest in the field. Aivars told us that he would leave the tall grass uncut until the birds migrated south later in the summer.

Sheltered beneath the roof of a large open shed was a season's supply of firewood, neatly split and stacked. I spied a solar water heater on the side of the house.

"That works all year?" I asked skeptically.

"Only in summer," Aivars admitted.

The garden this sunny morning was a still life waiting to be painted. The house was less artful. A conglomeration of scavenged glass, brick, concrete, and wood, that together created a sturdy structure of no apparent style.

Aivars directed us down a short flight of exterior stairs into his basement bread bakery, where for the next two hours I stood scribbling notes that I knew from experience would be difficult to decipher. I also wore a digital recorder around my neck. John did double duty, translating for me and taking photos with a small digital camera.

Of all the bakers I was to meet during this and other trips, Aivars was not the most technically gifted—not even close—but then and now he most embodied something quintessentially Latvian: the soulful veneration of Mother Earth and the heartfelt conviction that bread was her gift to humankind.

59. Rye Bread Tutorial

Jutting into the back wall of Aivars's basement was a large brick bread oven. Aivars built and later rebuilt the oven himself. Also in the back: A commercial kneading machine much the worse for wear. Aivars bought this device from a Russian merchant ship that was junking its equipment after the collapse of the former Soviet Union. Across from the oven was a wood-burning kitchen stove—adding hot water to flour speeds the fermentation process. On the other side: a collection of antique wooden paddles for sliding bread into and out of hot ovens, plus a variety of wooden spoons, wooden mixing bowls, and troughs, and a hodgepodge of barrels containing organic rye flour, as well as tall sacks overflowing with salt, caraway seed, and malt, the latter a sweetener made from sprouted rye and water that enhances the chemical reactions in bread dough, adding depth to the flavor.

One day a week Aivars baked a dozen oversized loaves of black-crusted *rupjmaize* in this kitchen. Some he gave away to family and friends; the rest he bartered for fresh produce, eggs, and an occasional slab of bacon.

As Aivars launched into his bread-baking spiel, with John translating, I focused on the sensory details. The grayish-brown color of whole-grain rye flour before it is baked—the black color of black bread comes from a chemical reaction known as the Maillard reaction that is accelerated when rye bread is baked in a hot oven. The chocolaty taste of the malt reminding me of the chocolate malt balls I devoured as a child.

Aivars told us that he stored his starter, made with rye flour and water—no wheat—in the freezer. That surprised me.

Starter is a living organism, a colony of bacteria that lives and breathes, defecates and reproduces, when kept in a congenial place and fed a diet of flour and water. Bakers often refrigerate their starters, but the freezer? Not so much. Noting my skepticism, Aivars reached into his refrigerator's freezer compartment and removed a plastic bucket. He dug out a spoonful of oatmeal-colored substance that resembled cookie dough for us to sample. I popped a piece in my mouth. No tang at all. "This batch is very sweet, maybe too sweet. It could be over the hill," Aivars said, returning the starter to the freezer. Sensing the sensitivity of the subject, I kept my critique of Aivars's starter to myself. The famed bread baker and cookbook writer Jeffrey Hamelman, the original director of Vermont's King Arthur bakery, later told me that he considered freezing the starter to be an offense against nature—Hamelman told me he stored his starter in his refrigerator, and he fed it several times a week. In this way he had kept it alive for nearly twenty years. Over time, he said, the flavor grew more nuanced and appealing, resulting in breads that were more complex and delicious. (Writing this book, I learned that many of the best professional bakers use both yeast and sourdough starter when baking bread: the starter promotes rising, yes, but its primary function is to enhance flavor.)

As the tutorial dragged on, I found myself wondering why the subjects I choose to write about invariably require the mastery of so much science. Bread baking begins with love and ends with love, but in the middle, there are acres of chemistry and physics to plow through. (The same was true of coffee.)

It was almost 1 p.m. when Aivars presented John and me

with a five-pound loaf with a dark crust that he had scored by hand—scoring marks are a baker's signature.

We crossed the street for lunch at a café and bar with picnic tables under a pergola. We picked an outside table and ordered Lāčplēsis, the local beer, now owned by Royal Unibrew, a Danish beverage company. The local chicken, Aivars said, was raised industrially, like chicken in the US, but the beef was grass-fed on a nearby farm, so we ordered small steaks. The meat was tough, but tasty. I was happy to let John and Aivars converse in Latvian while my brain took a rest.

60. Deprived

On a subsequent visit to Lielvārde, Aivars and I sat at his upstairs kitchen table, my pen and notebook and tape recorder before me. I began by asking if he, like John, grew up eating his mother's rye bread. Aivars waited a moment, then said, "My mother didn't bake bread. I didn't taste rye bread until I was nearly five years old."

How could that be?

When he was small, Aivars explained, there was no rupj-maize to be eaten. He had been born in Riga in August 1944, nine months before the end of the war. Small farmers—Stalin referred to them as "Latvian Kulaks"—were resisting the Red Army's effort to turn their farms into large collectives. The Russians won that fight, but the first phase of collectivization was a bust. Grain output declined. What little rye was available was requisitioned by the government and sent to state baker-ies that turned out so-called rye bread made with 70 percent wheat flour and 30 percent rye.

61. Aivars's Mother

Even if rye flour had been available, Aivars's mother, Anna, a city girl through and through, didn't know how to bake. Anna graduated from an elite high school in Riga, where she excelled in German. During the German occupation she worked as a bookkeeper and administrator of the Latvian Legion, the force of 140,000 Latvian men, conscripted (many against their will) by the Germans to fight the Russians on the eastern front. Because of her association with the Legion, when the Russians returned in 1944, they considered her to be a collaborator. As punishment, they sent her to live on a squalid state farm where milking cows was the only job open to her. There she lived for several years with Aivars, her only child, whose last name was the same as hers. As to the identity of Aivars's father? Was he a member of the Latvian Legion? A German officer? Pressed for details, Anna had little to say except, "It was wartime."

As to the first five years of Aivars's life: it was fortunate that he and his mother didn't starve to death. They lived in an unheated room in a bombed-out manor house with no running water. Their only nourishment was a pot of slop containing fatty meat, probably pork and potatoes. Morning, noon, and night the pot went from inside of the stove to the table. Like animals at a trough, they ate, then returned the pot to the stove until the next meal. And the next. And the next. Living in the cold and damp affected Aivars's lungs, and he suffered from other illnesses related to malnutrition.

In March and April of 1949, when the authorities were once again rounding up Latvians and shipping them to Siberia, Anna and some of her neighbors decided to send their children into hiding. The idea was to prevent the children from being deported, even if their parents were seized. Aivars, not yet five, was the youngest. The children moved every few days from one empty house to another—empty, because their male occupants had been deported to the labor camps in the gulag, while women and children had been sent to slightly less horrific "administrative settlements," also in Siberia. In one of these temporary houses, an adult provided the children with home-made *rupjmaize*. The memory of that bread shaped Aivars's destiny. "It was many years before I again tasted *rupjmaize*, but I never forgot. This bread was so sweet, and the good-ness lingered. I told myself someday I would learn to bake this bread."

62. Fulfilling His Fate

Anna was not sent to Siberia. She married, and her newly reconstituted family moved to a collective farm near Cēsis, northeast of Riga. There was more to eat at that farm, but conditions remained far from ideal. Rye bread baked in a state factory could be purchased there, but Aivars recalls it tasting of sawdust, which it no doubt contained. And Aivars's stepfather? A brain-injured vet who fought on the side of the Russians, he was both violent and alcoholic; but the fact that he had served in the Red Army improved Anna's political standing, making her eligible for a better-paying, more suitable job.

Help came from another source as well. Anna's father was a World War I war hero with a chest full of medals from his service with the Latvian Riflemen (Latviešu strēlnieki). This legendary band of pro-Bolshevik Latvian soldiers helped vault Lenin to power and served as his personal bodyguard. Aivars believes his grandfather, who worked as a party functionary enforcing political correctness at a glass factory, pulled strings to keep him and his mother out of Siberia. Aivars loved his grandfather and wanted to be like him. At age ten, when he proudly showed his grandfather his red bandana attesting to his membership in the Pioneers, his school's communist youth organization, Aivars was shocked by the older man's response.

"Son, don't get mixed up in that shit," his grandfather growled.

"But, grandfather," Aivars asked. "What about you? You're a communist."

"Yes, son," his grandfather answered, "I am the same kind of shit as the rest of them."

In 1961, when he was living in Cēsis with his mother and stepfather, Aivars's grandfather helped him gain entry into a four-year vocational boarding school, where students who excelled in sport ate well. (Athletic accomplishment was seen as bringing honor to the communist party and the Russian regime.) Aivars took up bicycle racing and skiing. The exercise and improved nutrition restored his lungs and turned him into an impassioned outdoorsman. Later he was admitted to a technical college, where he studied engineering part-time while working for the Merchant Marine.

For five years, Aivars worked as an engineer on a huge fishing vessel with an onboard canning factory. The ship was a self-contained world, remaining out at sea for months at a time, with, among other things, its own bakeries. Here Aivars learned to repair bread ovens, a skill that proved to be invaluable.

Ever cheerful and resourceful, Aivars did well at his job. After a few years a regional party boss offered to promote him to chief engineer for the entire fishing collective. Only thing: he would have to join the communist party. By now Aivars knew all about the party—its corruption and violence, and soul-destroying spying. If he didn't take the promotion and join the party, he was told, he would never work as a ship's engineer again.

So, he quit and went to work at a local waterworks. He tried to keep his head down, but his pride required him to work hard, and history repeated itself. A promotion was dangled before him, if only he would join the party. He quit the waterworks, and this time when he went looking for a job, he got lucky.

Landing in Lielvārde, he found a job collecting spare auto parts. His employer, *Lāčplēsis*, a huge agricultural and manufacturing collective run by a nominal communist with an entrepreneurial streak, exchanged the auto parts for potatoes. The collective, famous for its beer, wanted to start a bread bakery. It needed someone with engineering know-how to work with the architect designing and building the bread oven. Enter Aivars, a singular man with a passion for rye bread. The year was 1987.

Aivars spent two years building the collective's bread ovens and then, because no one else was interested, he became head baker. Like other bread bakers I met on my trips to Latvia, he sought advice and guidance from older people who remembered how bread had been baked prior to the advent of state-controlled Russian bread factories. By now the Soviet Union was on its last legs. The regime fell in 1991. Aivars managed to keep the *Lāčplēsis* rye bread bakery going until 1995. He tried to buy the bakery operation from the collective and take it private. But he had no stomach for the political maneuvering involved. Instead, Aivars took the money that was coming to him as a member of the *Lāčplēsis* collective and bought the property in Lielvārde where we visited him.

Here, irrepressible Candide that he is, Aivars built a house and a workshop where he repaired bread ovens. On the side, he grew organic fruits and vegetables and baked rye bread. On summer weekends he and his wife toured the countryside on their bicycles. In the winter, they skied. The economy was good. The economy was bad. The economy crashed. (Postcommunist Latvia was a very volatile place, both economically and politically.) In all seasons, Aivars was a happy man. His joyfulness and resilience helped him survive and even thrive following the death of his wife in a biking accident in 2012.

Aivars and his wife had been married for thirty-one years. Between them they had two daughters and two sons who produced many grandchildren with whom Aivars is close. Not one to live alone, Aivars met another woman with whom he shares his life today.

Avairs has known hardship and tragedy and encountered every sort of setback you can imagine and some you cannot.

Through it all, his energy and devotion have prevailed. "I love my family," Aivars says expansively. "And I love rye bread. Mine is a life filled with goodness."

63. *Lāči* Bread

We visited Normunds *Skauģis*, the exuberant proprietor of *Lāči*, Latvia's largest and most successful artisan bakery— in 2006, when John and his business partner started Black Rooster Food, it was *Lāči* that supplied them with *rupjmaize*. Normunds was born after the war into a once-prosperous family whose large farm had been seized and collectivized by the Russian government in the late 1940s. Luck and guile saved the *Skauģis* family from Siberia. Overhearing a party member whispering about an imminent roundup, Normunds's father acted quickly, hiding with his wife and children in an old barn until they could slip away after dark. For a number of years, they lived with relatives on a modest farm in a region too poor to interest the Russians, where Normunds's parents kept two cows—the legal limit. To earn money, Normunds's mother sold milk at a stand in Riga's vast Central Market. That was her licit product line. As to the illicit? Farmers were allowed to grow small amounts of rye for their own use. Whenever Normunds's mother was able to acquire a small stash of rye from a nearby farmer, she would bake a few loaves of *rupjmaize* that she carried to the market and hid under the counter. These she sold on the sly to customers deemed trustworthy, as if she were selling pot or moonshine. Even the most modest home bakers were not allowed to sell bread, lest they compete with state-owned bakeries. Unlike traditional rye breads, these officially-sanctioned loaves were baked in metal forms. Latvians dismissed them as "shaped bread," "pig bread," and "Stalin's cake."

When the former Soviet Union collapsed in 1991, Normunds applied to the newly formed Latvian government for the return of his family's property. Eventually his request was approved. A few years later, at great expense (by taking on a frightening amount of debt), he built a sprawling modern bakery on the grounds of the family farm. It paid off. With its world-class breads and pastries, its restaurants, souvenir shop, outdoor playground, free tours, and bread-making classes, *Lāči* quickly became one of the country's most popular tourist destinations.

As to his prize-winning *rupjmaize*, Normunds based his recipe on his mother's, and he used whole-grain flour milled from heirloom varietals of rye, as did other traditional Latvian home bakers. He diverted from the old way, however, by adding two pre-ferments to his dough, instead of one. *Lāči*'s pre-ferments, combining sourdough starter, water, and either rye flour or rye berries, were stored in large barrels on the bakery floor and left to ripen. When fully developed, the two pre-ferments were kneaded together simultaneously rather than sequentially with rye flour, water, salt, sugar, malt, and caraway to create a flavorful dough that was then left to rise. Later it was shaped by hand into loaves that were massaged with water and slipped into a top oven superheated to 900F. Once the crust was formed and the bread had sufficient structure, it was moved into a lower shelf and baked at a more moderate temperature.

(I did not understand the originality of *Lāči*'s dual-ferment rye bread technique until it was explained to me by our friend, the James Beard Award–winning baker Mark Furstenberg, who traveled to Latvia with John to learn about Latvian rye bread. "John told me the bread in Riga was baked at nine hundred degrees Fahrenheit. I simply didn't believe him," Mark later recalled. "I wanted to see baking that I knew nothing about." According to Mark, Normunds's "non-linear" practice of adding two well-rested pre-ferments simultaneously is technically innovative, and it produces dough that is complex and deeply flavorful.)

64. What We Crave
"*Rupjmaize* is not a gourmet food," a Latvian relative told me in exasperation after reading an early draft of this book. "*Rupjmaize* is not the only bread we eat. It's the food we crave when we have been away from home for too long."

65. Solstice 1
We coordinated the dates of our trip in 2010 so we would be in Latvia for the summer solstice.

66. Solstice 2
Since seed was first sown and grain first cultivated, humans have associated the long daylight hours of midsummer with fecundity. On the longest day of the year, ancient peoples from grain-growing regions throughout Europe celebrated the early summer's sexual urgency.

Pagan customs related to the summer solstice persisted in Northern Europe long after the arrival of Christianity—Shakespeare's *A Midsummer Night's Dream*, written in the sixteenth century, and Ingmar Bergman's *Smiles of a Summer Night* (on which the Sondheim musical *A Little Night Music* is based), written and produced in the mid-twentieth, both have as their underlying theme sexual anarchy breaking loose during the year's shortest night. Well into the modern era, the bonfires that burned on solstice eve were understood to bestow fertility on plants, animals, and humans. In service of this seasonal fecundity, Latvian dainas urged young couples to enter the woods hand-in-hand on Midsummer Night searching for a mythical night-blooming fern. This pagan message was delivered in defiance of church fathers. In an effort to suppress midsummer's juicier aspects, early Christian prelates began associating the holiday with the June 24th birth of John the Baptist—the solstice occurs either on June 21 or June 22. In Latvia, this campaign led to midsummer being renamed Jāņi, or Jāņu diena (St. John's Day.) Even today Latvians, Christian and not, refer to Midsummer Eve as Jāņi. My own Jāņi predictably refuses to refer to the solstice by its Christianized name. With his anticlerical bias, he proves himself a worthy descendant of his distant relative Emīls Melngailis, an ethno-musicologist who in 1900 published a collection of midsummer songs and took credit for introducing *Līgo svētki*, a non-Christianized term for midsummer.

67. Jāņi, Jāņi Afrikāņi

The week before we departed for Latvia, John photocopied scores of his favorite midsummer dainas. These, along with his 2009 oak wreath (wingspan approximately two feet), he packed in his suitcase, it being the custom for men to throw last year's wreath into this year's fire—oak trees symbolize male virility and strength. John imagined himself with a new hand-stitched wreath of oak perched on his head, singing folk songs all night long. (In Latvia, at midsummer the sun sets at 10 p.m. and rises at 4 a.m. but the sky, magically, never fully darkens.) The solstice embodied all that John loved best in his heritage: the rural setting, the singing and revelry, the folk songs, and the rules-defying tie to the pagan past.

One part of John's dream did come true that summer: he did throw his old wreath into the bonfire. Beyond that, little went according to script.

On Midsummer Eve, John and I joined a contingent of family and friends at Latvia's outdoor Ethnographic Open-Air Museum, located on a lake on the outskirts of Riga. The party wasn't exactly what John had envisioned. Latvian culture as remembered by John and other exiles in America is preserved as a relic. The young Latvians with whom we partied that night had little interest in fossilized custom. Rather than folk musicians in linen folk costumes playing handmade folk instruments and singing ancient folk songs, the musicians featured that night were members of a reggae band led by a young, talented mixed-race Latvian musician who replaced the traditional "Līgo, Līgo" reprise of Latvian midsummer songs celebrated by Emīls Melngailis with the reggae-inspired refrain "Jāņi, Jāņi Afrikāņi."

The musical diversity testified to the tremendous eagerness of young, post-Soviet Latvians to connect with the world at large. Latvia faces west across the Baltic and young people there were and are tremendously interested in all that is new and innovative in the West. New forms of music. New forms of media and visual art. New types of food. This openness to the greater world felt congenial to me. It was easy for me to connect with young people who shared my delight in the new.

John, however, was heartbroken. He had waited so long to return to Latvia for the summer solstice. Perhaps he had waited too long.

68. Indra Čekstere and the Blue-Eyed Baker

Eager to immerse ourselves in the history of rye bread baking in Latvia, John and I made plans to meet up with the anthropologist and bread scholar Indra Čekstere at a bread festival in Gauja National Park on July 25—Saint Jacob's Day, the traditional start of the rye harvest. Čekstere, employed as a folklorist by the National Park, had dreamed up the festival seven years earlier to interest Latvians, especially Latvian children, in their heritage, and she had been running it ever since. The year we visited, some 700 adults and children participated in the fete, which took place in a large open fairground beneath a Dutch-style forty-foot windmill built in the mid-nineteenth century that had once belonged to the local baronial estate. (In this, Čekstere was playing a bit fast and loose—the beautifully renovated windmill was not, strictly speaking, a Latvian cultural artifact.)

Windmill notwithstanding, at the time, Čekstere probably knew more about Latvian bread making and the folklore surrounding it than any person alive. Earlier in the year, I had read her book *Mūsu Maize: Our Daily Bread,* a picturesque accounting of bread-making practices, traditions, customs, and beliefs in Latvia's various regions. (Despite its small size, Latvia is geographically and culturally diverse.) Hundreds of women, middle-aged and old, a good number born before World War II, had provided Čekstere with enough information to understand the material culture associated with Latvian bread-making, as well as the folklore.

It was hot and sunny when John and I arrived, and a folk concert and a folk-dance exhibition were already underway. The scene we encountered seemed as if it had been lifted from the pages of Čekstere's book: Matrons in linen dirndls wearing wreaths made of rye, rye stalks encircling their faces. Girls in woven red skirts (members of the folk chorus), wreaths of summer flowers on their heads. Young men beating handmade wooden drums. Boys tooting wooden flutes. A dozen contestants (including our friend Aivars) stood at wooden tables slicing up loaves of *rupjmaize* to be sampled by the judges. Čekstere, in her fifties, with whitish-blondish hair, her pale skin turned ruddy by the sun, stood at the center of the action in a long skirt, holding a microphone.

Following the competition, the crowd increased by many hundred. There was food for sale. Activities. Music. We toured the windmill, then strolled through a parking lot filled with artisans, bakers, and chefs offering their wares. After that, we followed a small crowd of children carrying worksheets as they traversed "the Loaf's path," designed to teach them the many steps involved in the process of making bread. Children who finished the course were given a free pancake, which struck me as slightly tone-deaf.

As the afternoon wore on, we realized that this event was more aspirational than historic. In the old days, Saint Jacob's Day did indeed mark the harvesting of the first rye, but there had been no Saint Jacob's Day Festival. Čekstere had designed this event to reintroduce urbanized Latvians to folk traditions that had been under siege since the Soviets occupied Latvia, and to encourage the public to see the lasting value of these local and regional traditions.

And the competition cemented the shift: the winner was not a granny in a linen dirndl. The winner was a guy in his late thirties or early forties. A handsome, muscular fellow in a sleeveless black leather shirt and black leather pants with shoulder-length black hair, skin tanned dark, and dazzling sapphire eyes. The winning baker had ridden into town on a Suzuki motorcycle accompanied by four other similarly clad motorcycle dudes. A construction worker by trade, he told me he had figured out how to modify the electric oven in his home to make it hotter—thereby ensuring a dark and gleaming crust. To learn bread baking, he read a book and then consulted with local elders. In that sense, Čekstere's festival accomplished precisely what she set out to do: encouraging a younger generation of Latvians to reach out to older countrymen and -women in order to keep their country's bread-making traditions alive.

69. Peter Reinhart

I returned home mulling over what I had learned about rye bread as a food and as a cultural artifact. The summer had made me realize how little I knew about the history of bread and its multiple symbolic meanings. A friend suggested I download Peter Reinhart's TED Talk exploring bread's intangibles. Reinhart is a baker, a teacher of bakers, and a prize-winning writer—his 2007 book about whole-grain breads won a James Beard Award, as did two other cookbooks written by him. Reinhart began mastering the art of bread baking in the 1970s as a lay brother in an Eastern Orthodox service order in northern California—there he baked bread both for the joy of it and to fulfill the religious obligation to feed the poor. Though he later left the religious order, Reinhart held on to his sense of bread as spiritually charged and transformational. He and his wife, Susan, founded Brother Juniper's Café and Bakery in Forestville, California, in 1986—one of the first artisan bakeries in what was to become the country's most bread-centric state. In his TED Talk Reinhart described bread's four levels of meaning. He began with the literally caloric—bread as the staff of life. The food on which ordinary people subsist. (In Europe, well into the modern age, bread and cereal provided the poor with the majority of their daily calories.) Next Reinhart spoke of bread's metaphorical meaning. We know the world through bread. We earn our bread and butter. We break bread with friend and foe. He talked about bread's ethical dimension. Humans have an ethical and moral obligation to provide the poor with their daily bread. Ignoring that injunction violates the principles of every religion. And finally, he spoke about bread as an object of religious mystery. In Christianity, by consuming the communion wafer, worshippers are transformed, becoming one with the body of Christ. In the Jewish faith, the manna God bestowed on his people as they wandered in the desert did more than satisfy their hunger—it created an unbreakable covenant between them. This notion of bread as mysterious and the gift of God or, prior to monotheism, the gods, is as old as bread itself, predating Christianity and Judaism and indeed most other modern religions by thousands of years.

70. Holy and Eternal

"Holy and eternal is bread. It keeps you from hunger and misery. The Creator himself gave it to us. He who dishonors bread dishonors life itself."—Sign painted on a wall at the headquarters of the Berlin Bakers' Guild.

71. On the Couch. In the Lab. At the Museum.

Bread, in fact, has more than four meanings. There is, for example, the psychoanalytic meaning: bread as a stand-in for the mother's breast. In this frame of reference, biting into a slice of bread can be interpreted as an act of cannibalism. That idea is not so preposterous when you consider the idea shared by prehistoric peoples of grain as a gift spontaneously bursting from Mother Earth's fertile womb. This thinking is abetted by biology: grains are fast-evolving and fast-growing grasses that come to us unbidden. Where there was little, soon there is enough to feed multitudes. What could be more mysterious and awe-inducing?

On the other end of the spectrum is the scientific and technological meaning of *bread*: as the product of prodigiously complex chemical, physical, and biological reactions that require intensive laboratory observation and study. It is this scientific approach that informs Nathan Myhrvold's five-volume, over-2,300-page tome, *Modernist Bread*, published in 2017.

Feeding aesthetic hungers is yet another way of finding meaning in a hand-crafted loaf. The TikTok and Instagram trend of using fresh vegetables and herbs to create edible focaccia art, or "breadscapes," is new, but not new. Since before the time of Christ, painters and sculptors have felt compelled to depict the process and product of bread making. (If you have trouble swallowing all this philosophizing about bread, think about the tens of millions of people who pondered the intricacies of sourdough starter during the first year of the COVID-19 pandemic. As surely as bread rises, ordinary people since time immemorial have found wondrous meaning in the metamorphosis of grain and water in the presence of heat.)

72. The Museum of Bread Culture (2012)

Čekstere had spent time at the Museum of Bread Culture in Ulm, Germany, and her description of the museum triggered my curiosity. We decided to visit on our next trip to Europe. Our three-day stay in Ulm in 2012 was mind-opening. After touring the museum and talking at length with its director, Dr. Andrea Fadani, my vague awareness that bread and its absence drove human history clicked into sharp focus. Just as the rising price of flour in late eighteenth-century France triggered bloody revolution in that country, so it had been throughout history in cereal-growing and -eating regions.

The Museum of Bread Culture was founded and endowed in 1955 by father-and-son industrialists, Willy and Hermann Eiselin, in order to explain and explore the connection between famine and war. The Eiselins grew wealthy selling baking supplies in their native Germany. Both had served in the German military—Willy in World War I, Hermann in World War II. Their experiences as soldiers turned them into pacifists. They used their fortune to support scientific research and to create a museum that would teach Germans, especially German children, and all the world, the way bread had shaped—and continues to shape—human history. (Russia's 2022 blockades of Ukrainian ports, delaying and in some cases preventing passage of Ukrainian wheat to starving populations in Africa and Asia, provides yet another tragic example of this phenomena.)

Housed in a historic building near Ulm's soaring cathedral, the museum's permanent collection is a treasure trove for scholars. It includes over six thousand books and hundreds of paintings, from old masters to German expressionists, along with other artworks related to bread and bread-making. Among its holdings: a small six-thousand-year-old sculpture from ancient Egypt depicting a woman on her knees, hand-milling grain that would later be used to bake bread. The museum's permanent collection culminated in a series of rooms displaying original drawings, posters, and other kinds of materials from the 1930s that were designed to fuel the German people's fear of going without bread. Created by Hitler's propagandists, these posters illustrate the Fuhrer's oft-repeated (false) assertion that Jews, most especially Jewish grain merchants, caused the traumatic famine in Germany following World War I. In this way, the fear of hunger, that most primal of fears, was manipulated by Hitler to enflame anti-Semitic hatred, thus furthering his agenda, and helping him vault to power.

73. H. E. Jacob

The Eiselins were inspired to create their museum after reading the book that bread scholar William Rubel described to me in an email as "the preeminent work on the history of bread." H. E. Jacob, a popular German Jewish scholar and journalist, arrested by the Nazis in 1938 and imprisoned in Dachau and Buchenwald, wrote *Six Thousand Years of Bread* after fleeing to America in 1939. Published in 1944, the book is a mesmerizing, poetical deep dive into the history of bread. Jacob believed bread originated in ancient Egypt six thousand years ago. Recent scholarship has gone beyond what was known in Jacob's time without erasing the book's impact, its charm, or the accuracy of its understanding of bread's primacy in history and culture.

74. William Rubel (2015)

Some years after our visit to Ulm, John and I traveled to Santa Cruz, California to spend a few days with Bill Rubel, the bread scholar with whom I corresponded and the author of a small introduction to bread with a large name, *Bread: A Global History*. John and I were eager to talk with him about Latvian rye bread—as always, we traveled with samples. Another of Rubel's books, *The Magic of Fire*, is about hearth cooking. He made dinner for us, roasting a chicken in the traditional bee-hive oven he had built in his backyard. Rubel collects antique cooking utensils: he prepared the chicken, along with some potatoes and an onion, in a 500-year-old footed iron vessel from France—the feet enabled the heat to circulate freely under and around the pot, speeding the cooking time. We ate dinner outdoors in his garden, a good choice, given a level of domestic disorder associated with genius and the cluck-clucking chick-ens going in and out of the kitchen.

For the last dozen years Rubel has been researching and writing a not-yet-published work that he expects to be the definitive worldwide history of bread. Already he has written thousands of pages, and still his work is nowhere near com-pletion. As with virtually all fields of study, technological advances in the last fifty years have radically altered scholars' understanding of bread's relationship to the past.

75. Research 1

Take, for example, the way advances in scientific imaging, car-bon dating, and DNA analysis of bones and fossils have altered what we know about bread consumption. Samples gathered at prehistoric sites in Italy, Russia, and the Czech Republic have established that "starch grains," possibly in the form of flour, were staples of the human diet over 30,000 years ago. Significant evidence has emerged, thanks to these technologies, proving, for example, that hunters and gatherers who lived in the Mid-Upper Paleolithic era collected wild grain that they ground on flat stones and probably cooked. In other words, those late Paleolithic cave dwellers painting gloriously abstract animal figures on cave walls were not just catch-as-catch-can hunter-gatherers: it appears they ate a more varied diet, one that included processed grains, as well as fruits, vegetables, and meat.

76. Research 2

Thousands of years after our human ancestors added grain in some form to their diets, rye popped up in the Fertile Crescent as an unwelcome weed in fields of barley, einkorn, and other early cultivars of wheat. Rye is a grass like no other: able to grow in frigid temperatures and poor soil, amid cycles of drought and drench—moreover, its deep roots protect the earth and discourage competing weeds from growing in fields where it is cultivated. When the earth entered a period of severe global cooling 12,000 years ago, rye became an important source of food in the Fertile Crescent. When the earth warmed and people in that region returned to eating wheat, rye migrated toward cooler climes. Its journey to Europe and Russia continued for thousands of years, aided by the invention and adoption of the iron sickle. This tool for cutting wheat paradoxically caused the production of rye to soar by inadvertently disseminating rye seeds. By the late Middle Ages, rye was a staple crop in regions of Spain and France, the British Isles, Switzerland, Germany, Poland, central Europe, the Baltics, Scandinavia, and Russia. West of Germany, wheat was generally the favored grain, although breads often contained both wheat and rye. Bread made exclusively with rye was often dismissed by Western Europeans as food for dumb beasts and peasants. Reading Bill Rubel's *Bread* book, I learned that in England four hundred years ago, rye flour, bran, and waste from the bakery floor were baked into a dense, flat bread—called horse bread—that was fed to animals (and sometimes eaten by the poorest of the poor humans). The existence of horse bread may well have fueled the folktale that Napoleon's horse Nicole was a rye bread eater, leading imaginative folks to suggest that *pain pour Nicole* ("bread for Nicole") was the original pumpernickel—a bit far-fetched, that one.

In lands where little wheat was grown, such as Scandinavia and the Baltics and parts of Russia, anti-rye prejudice did not exist. For hundreds of years in this part of the world, the rye trade shaped the economy. Peasants living in colder, wetter climates worshipped at the altar of rye, as their counterparts in France revered wheat.

77. Taking Rye to Its Limit

"There is something primal about the rye breads of Russia and the Baltics," wrote scholar and baker Stanley Ginsberg, in his wonderful book *The Rye Baker*. These breads "are dark and dense, intensely sour, infused with the musky, chocolaty sweetness of malted rye . . ." They "take rye to its limit."

As to the rye breads of John's homeland, Ginsberg wrote, "of all the [rye] breads of Eastern Europe, the breads of Latvia are held in highest regard." The best of Latvian breads were so outstandingly delicious that in his opinion they required nothing to showcase their perfection, not even butter. (On this point, I respectfully disagree. While bowing to Mr. Ginsberg's double genius as rye baker and rye scholar, I prefer my Latvian rye bread with sweet butter.)

78. Bread of Our Fathers

It pleased me to think that John's ancestors in Latvia and mine in Belarus ate the same kind of rye bread back in the day. This idea made sense, given the geographical proximity and climatological similarity of Latvia and Belarus, and it was confirmed by my reading of memoirs and novels. But I am not fluent in Yiddish or Russian. Stanley Ginsberg reads both these languages and more. When diving into *The Rye Baker* and his earlier book, *Inside the Jewish Bakery,* I was gratified to discover that his research supported my supposition.

Ginsberg grew up in Brooklyn in the 1950s, where he ate Americanized rye bread containing more wheat than rye. (This facsimile rye exemplified the postwar industrialization of foods favored by immigrants.) Ginsberg was amazed, therefore, when researching rye bread in Eastern Europe, to discover "a deeper layer of rye baking," one that produced an entirely different kind of rye bread. Ginsberg concluded that "dense, intensely flavored black breads [had] sustained my grandparents and their grandparents in the villages and towns of Eastern Europe."

Elsewhere, Ginsberg quoted a Yiddish historian describing the bread eaten by the poor Jews of Drohitchin, a shtetl in the western corner of Belarus near Poland: "The rye bread could stay good for weeks, and the older it got, the tastier and more delicious it became."

Just like the *rupjmaize* that stayed fresh in our bread drawer for weeks.

79. Jewish Hunger

In Abraham Cahan's autobiographical novel, *The Rise of David Levinsky*, published in 1917, the author described the omnipresence of hunger in the lives of Russian Jews. Cahan's alter ego, David Levinsky, and his widowed mother lived in a squalid basement room with three other families in the shtetl of Antomir. There they survived on pennies a day. In such a life, Cahan wrote, "a hunk of rye bread and a bit of herring or cheese" separated the living from the dead. Crowded in dank misery, the women squabbled as their hungry children nagged: "Mamma, I want a piece of bread." Cahan depicted their mothers responding angrily: "Again bread! You'll eat my head off. May the worms eat you." *The Rise of David Levinsky* is a novel, not a memoir. Still, the idea of a Jewish mother begrudging her children food astonished me. And yet when the cupboard was bare, of course there was anger.

80. Alfred Kazin 2

The academically gifted literary critic Alfred Kazin—whose desperate pursuit of perfect grades reminded me of John— was born in Brooklyn in 1915 to immigrant parents who grew up in circumstances similar to those described by Cahan in his novel. Kazin and his friends, poor though their families were, never went hungry. Not even close. In *A Walker in the City*, Kazin wrote about his youth in Brownsville, Brooklyn, a working-class neighborhood crowded with immigrants, where

Jewish parents, reacting perhaps to life in the old country, routinely overfed their offspring. According to Kazin, children "never had a chance to know what hunger meant." Kazin recalls his mother extorting him: "Eat! Eat!" And if he failed to comply? "May you be destroyed if you don't eat." So eat young Alfred did: all day, every day. Even playing in the street with his friends, the author remembers interrupting the "grimmest punchball game" to shout up to his mother, asking her to "hoist down at the end of a clothesline, thick slices of rye bread smeared with chicken fat."

81. Jewish Rye Bread in America

You may be surprised to learn that rye bread's roots in America were not Jewish. German gentiles, not Jews, introduced rye bread in New York City in the mid-1800s and popularized it in the decades that followed. Germans were among the first occupants of the tenement buildings on Manhattan's Lower East Side, where Jews and other immigrants later lived. Germans left their mark on these buildings, installing bread ovens in the basements and building out small bakery storefronts on the first floor. In the late nineteenth century, there could be as many as two or three tenement bakeries per block featuring different kinds of rye and whole-grain breads. By 1908 or 1909, when my grandmother Hannah would have visited her relatives on the Lower East Side, most German immigrants had moved uptown, but their bakeries remained. Walking down the street, my grandmother would have inhaled the fragrance of fresh rye bread wafting up through metal grates from innumerable basement bakeries.

82. Leon Swell

In the fall of 2012, I attended a Bread Guild master class in rye bread baking in Charlotte, North Carolina. There I met a professional baker who told me about her father, a retired biochemist then in his mid-eighties, who fell in love with rye bread as a small boy in New York City. The idea of talking with an enthusiast who'd been around during rye's New York heyday intrigued me, and I arranged to talk to him on the phone.

Born in 1927, Leon Swell grew up in a largely Jewish working-class neighborhood in the West Bronx, where "bread" meant rye bread. None of the many bakeries located in a three or four block radius of his house sold what Swell called white bread—although they did sell challah and bagels.

Among the breads Swell remembered eating as a child were a lightly soured, soft grayish loaf with a shiny crust and caraway seeds. (A version of the classic "Jewish deli rye," available to this day in bakeries and delis such as Zingerman's in Ann Arbor, Michigan, and, of course, Zabar's.) Another bread Swell loved was a dense, moist "corn rye." It contained no corn—the name came from the Yiddish *kornbroyt*, or "grain bread." Favored by Jews from parts of Lithuania and Poland, kornbroyt was baked in large boules and sold by the pound. Both these ryes went well with the pastrami and tongue that Swell's mother bought home as special treats.

Swell came of age when bakers still worked through the night in subterranean chambers. He believes rye bread was produced underground, but it's the bagel-making he remembers. Swell worked as delivery boy. On Saturday nights his boss sent him to buy bagels on a street "dotted with iron grates."

Picking up one of these grates, Swell saw "a world of bakeries underneath the sidewalk" where wood-burning hearths cast mysterious light on "men in white hats, five or six to a room, working in front of tubs of boiling water," where bagels were "dunked to give them their shiny coat then fished out with wooden paddles . . ."

As to the rye breads that were his daily fare, Swell remembers a third kind he didn't like very much. This was "a very sour, very coarse pumpernickel sold in a five-pound loaf," that most likely contained both wheat and rye flours. Swell's father bought this "pumpernickel" at a bakery on the Lower East Side near his work called Moshers, where the bakers brought their sourdough cultures with them from Germany and elsewhere when they emigrated to New York.

The pumpernickel Leon Swell described appears to have had little in common with the two pumpernickel recipes in Stanley Ginsberg's *The Rye Bake*—not the Westphalian one that appears on the cover nor the soft Americanized pumpernickel with raisins that calls for caramel and other food colorings to achieve its dark brown hue. Fact is: pumpernickel in America is a pretty squishy term—hence the older gentlemen in Zabars insisting to me that Latvian *rupjmaize* is pumpernickel. As to the presence of California raisins in American-style pumpernickel: *New York Times* columnist R. W. Apple claimed that innovation was introduced by Louis Orwasher in 1945 when he returned to his family's bakery on East 78th Street in Manhattan after serving as a baker in the US Army. Founded in 1916, Orwashers Bakery still exists, although bakers no longer work in the basement. You can still buy pumpernickel there. The present version is made with unbleached rye flour, rye flakes (from the kernels or berries of the rye), and no raisins.

83. My Brooklyn

The shopping district in the Bronx where Leon Swell's mother pulled her shopping cart in and out of one small store after another was similar to the Bensonhurst neighborhood of Brooklyn where my grandmother lived. When visiting her in the mid-1950s, how charmed I was as a child by the endless variety of stores. Among them, two bread bakeries (one Jewish and one Italian); two cake bakeries (one Jewish and one Italian); a delicatessen selling kosher deli meats; an appetizing store selling smoked fish, where my grandmother told the counterman she wanted a special piece of hot smoked salmon "cut from the center because my children are visiting" (and, yes, I still wonder who got the ends of the salmon); a Syrian candy store selling sesame candy and halvah; a fish store with living fish circling in a tank—you picked out the fish you wanted and the fishmonger bonked it on the head with a wooden mallet; a poultry store where the counterman plucked the feathers off your chicken after he wrung its neck; and the butcher shop where I first knew love (I had a crush on the butcher). Not to be forgotten: the so-called "candy store" that was really a newspaper store, with an indoor soda fountain and outdoor newspaper rack. On the way to the subway, you were allowed to grab a paper and keep going, dropping your coins on the counter in front of the window as you passed by. You ventured inside the candy store's dark interior for one reason alone: to order a foaming delight called a chocolate egg cream containing Fox's u-bet Chocolate Flavor Syrup and seltzer and no egg and no cream. It was here, in Brooklyn, that I fell in love with cities and became a foodie and future food writer.

That Brooklyn was superior to the Boston suburb where I lived in car-driven comfort, I never doubted. Who wouldn't prefer shopping in Brooklyn to the boring old Elm Farm supermarket where once a week my mother bought bread wrapped in plastic and unadorned chocolate chip cookies (could anything compare with the icing on a black-and-white cookie bought at a Brooklyn bakery?) along with lamb chops and whole chickens and bags of potatoes for mashing.

As to rye bread in Bensonhurst? My grandmother ate Jewish deli rye from the bakery that she insisted on buying without seeds because caraway got under her false teeth. That's how they sold rye bread in Brooklyn. With seeds and without. I preferred a pretzel roll with a lot of salt. Or a bagel. Or a black-and-white cookie.

Rye bread, I could take it or leave it.

84. Jewish Food-Joy.

My stout, bosomy, tightly corseted, irrepressible grandmother was the source in our family of what Jane Ziegelman, director of the culinary program at New York City's Tenement Museum described in her book, *97 Orchard,* as "Jewish food-joy." Jews, Ziegelman wrote, "came to the dinner table with a distinct and highly developed zest for eating." Like their fondness for fat, Zeigelman opined, this enthusiasm was born in scarcity, but went far beyond. Jewish food-joy, she wrote was grounded "in the elaborate system of culinary laws and rituals that transformed the everyday business of eating into a sacred act." Acknowledging food's sacredness, she wrote, was the core belief of Jewish food culture, "always simmering in the Jewish eater's thoughts." Every week on the Sabbath, Jews enacted their ideas about the holiness of the table, sharing a ritual dinner at which they celebrated "nothing less than the miracle of creation."

Ziegelman's conjecture that Jewish food-joy is rooted in a form of religious practice that requires limitation and restraint makes some sense, but I doubt it tells the whole story. I suspect that the geographic origins of ancient Hebrews may have played a part in instilling food-joy in Jewish hearts. Jews migrated to the cold, wet clime of Eastern Europe from temperate regions located on or near the Mediterranean, including the Fertile Crescent, Spain, and medieval France. Food-joy, Jewish and otherwise, abounds in these lands. One needs only browse Claudia Roden's *The Book of Jewish Food*, with its sumptuous recipes featuring Middle Eastern spice mixtures, and ingredients, or Joan Nathan's surprising exploration of French Jewish cuisine, *Quiches, Kugels, and Couscous*, to know that Jewish food, and no doubt Jewish attitudes toward food, are rooted, at least partially, in regions and cultures that know and celebrate abundance.

85. Overdoing It

Whatever the reason, Jews in America are known for their culinary excess. The food historian Hasia R. Diner chalks it up to a reenactment of the thrill bedazzled newcomers experienced when they arrived on these shores at the turn of the century and discovered that humble laborers ate meat every day, and wheat flour for baking cake and challah cost no more than rye flour. In other words, poor people in America ate better than the rich in the old country.

When confronted with our tendency to overdo, generations of Jewish women—including me and my friends—respond with words so predictable they function as an incantation: "God forbid there isn't enough food." We deliver this line as if scarcity represents an immediate threat against which God must protect us. After uttering these words, the speaker and her companions—by which I mean my friends and I—recognizing our folly, invariably laugh.

86. Zaftig

When first- and second-generation Jewish *fressers*—"enthusiastic eaters," in Yiddish—sat down to one of those mile-high meat sandwiches for which New York Jewish delis were so famous in the second half of the twentieth century, they wanted their meat contained by slices of firm, tangy rye that would not fall apart, what with the spicy mustard and coleslaw and Russian dressing and all that fat oozing from the meat.

Given this cultural embrace of excess, it is not surprising that Jewish women were often described as *zaftig*, the Yiddish word for "juicy" or "succulent." Zaftig was a semi-okay way to be in Marilyn Monroe's mid-century America, but by the time I was a teenager, the cultural ideal of thinness had transformed

Jewish-American women into some of the diet industry's most enthusiastic adherents—Weight Watchers was founded by a Jewish woman, Jean Nidetch, whose maiden name of Slutsky raises the possibility that her family may have come from the same shtetl—Slutsk—as my grandmother Hannah.

Which brings us back to the revisionist lesson that I, a second-generation Jewish American girl, learned from my mother, an inveterate dieter who loved good food and baked sublime Danish pastries, Nesselrode tartlets, and apple pies. It should be noted that there were no New York–style Jewish bakeries in the Massachusetts town where I grew up. At the one and only New York–style Jewish deli in our area, Jack and Marion's in Brookline, an establishment flashy enough for the Las Vegas strip, the pastrami was divine, but in my memory the rye bread was nothing to write home about. My mother treated our bread desert as an opportunity: When you go out on a date, she coached me, order a roast beef sandwich (not fatty pastrami), slather it with mustard and coleslaw, use a knife and fork to cut the meat, and leave the bread on your plate. You can eat the pickle. My mother taught me this lesson in bread aversion in the mid-sixties, at the same time that John's mother labored in her kitchen kneading *rupjmaize* to feed the souls and bodies of her hungry men. In my family, bread—rye or wheat—had become the enemy as it continues to be for many gluten-fearing, carbohydrate-loathing American women and men, Jewish and gentile. This trend persists today, but its opposite is also gaining popularity as bread is rebirthed by a new generation of bakers using heirloom varieties of whole grains milled in small batches.

But now comes the kicker. Please raise a glass of Dr. Brown's Cel-Ray soda in recognition of the fact that I, an heir of Jewish-American bread fear, married the Emperor of Latvian Rye Bread, and in so doing, I discovered my love of the kind of toothsome, nutritious rye that kept our ancestors alive a hundred years ago, and in this way I was transformed. If that's too optimistic an ending, let's say I was sort of transformed.

87. A Rationing Mentality

Food-joy in the Jewish sense is not a Latvian thing. John's love of food—and he does love food—is tempered by a reflexive restraint that many Balts and Scandinavians share. This cautious approach to consumption developed in a natural environment where the growing season is short and only a relatively limited number of fruits, grains, legumes, and vegetables grow. His reticence may also reflect what the geographer and all-round deep thinker Edmunds Bunkše has described as "the Latvian distaste for drama and hyperbole."

Farming, not to mention surviving, in northern climes breeds stoicism. In the early years of our marriage, I had a hard time understanding John's ability to restrain himself and delay gratification. It was unthinkable that he would ruin his appetite grazing, while I—well, if I had just come in from swimming or hiking, or even if I hadn't, sometimes I ate the equivalent of dinner while I was making dinner. The Swedish ethnologist and food historian Richard Tellström helped me understand the Nordic self-limiting impulse when he wrote that a "rationing mentality" regulated everyday eating and cooking in Sweden.

A rationing mentality. Less is more. Waste is a sin. Saving for tomorrow is a high virtue. And abundance? Well, most times of the year abundance can make a food-rationing person uncomfortable. But then comes a time when feasting and restraint gives way to celebration. At seasonal fêtes such as Christmas (or the winter solstice) and Midsummer Festival, holding back gives way to "extravagant partying," says Tellström. This habit of feast or famine mimics the way of life of prehistoric hunters and gatherers who gorged on meat when animals were killed and then survived on greens and grains, but there is a difference: In Northern Europe, the habit of restraint may have begun due to circumstances, but it has become ingrained—now there's a word—in culture and in individual psyches.

Oh, one more thing about Tellström. It was in his introductory essay to Magnus Nilsson's *The Nordic Cookbook* where I first came across the phrase "bread with an old-soul" to describe the grainy loaves that were the staple food in northeastern Europe for millennia. The intuitive intermingling of the culinary and the spiritual in this phrase could not be more on point: in Latvia, in the Baltic, in Scandinavia, and in Russia, rye bread is understood to feed the body, yes, and also feed the soul.

88. Offspring

Funny about children. The way they replicate parts of yourself it never occurred to you to think of as heritable. All three of our children love food and hospitality: qualities they share with us and with Liz, John's ex-wife. There are differences, though, among the offspring. Like me, Noah possesses an abundance of Jewish food-joy. Like me, he is a meat lover. Like John, Ilze and Sarma's love of food is tempered by restraint. Neither Ilze nor Sarma eat meat. Sarma, in fact, is mostly vegan.

89. Paradigm Shift

Marketing Latvian rye bread established John as a kind of cultural ambassador and tireless advocate of Latvian bread. As for me, the years I spent researching and writing this book added warmth to my feelings about Latvia and Latvians and it seemed to change how some Latvian Americans perceived me.

90. History Is a Bitch

We traveled to Latvia numerous times in search of John's roots. My own roots in Eastern Europe I largely ignored until 2012, when, prior to visiting Latvia, I arranged for us to tour Lithuania with a guide well versed in Jewish history.

Talking with friends about this planned journey, I noticed a certain discomfort in the room. I felt pushed to state where my deepest loyalties lay: if my companions were Jewish, they wanted me to proclaim out loud that Jews suffered more than any other group during World War II. That they did, seemed to me indisputable: among rational people, there is no denying the six million dead, no denying that Hitler largely succeeded in annihilating European Jewry. If they were Latvian or Latvian American, they often wanted me to admit that Latvia's lesser-known Holocaust, the one carried out by Stalin, was as bad as, maybe worse than, the Jewish Holocaust. Making such a comparison struck me as wrong, but I did not say so. Instead,

I spoke of "dueling holocausts" and dueling victimologies. "History is a bitch, and everyone suffers." That was my standard answer. By saying that I was acknowledging the vastness of human suffering. If pressed, I would say that every smashed skull was its own holocaust. I believed that to be true before delving into my own family's history and I still believe it to be true. There are, however, many truths, and all are not equal.

91. Litvaks

I, too, had a tribe.

Growing up in a WASP bastion adjacent to Cambridge, Massachusetts, my mother told me that we, by which she meant the maternal side of my family, were Litvaks, so-called "Russian Jews" from Lithuania, Belarus, and other areas on the western edge of Czarist Russia. In my mother's version of history, we Litvaks were the superior Eastern European Jews. Our version of the Jewish religion, she said, emphasized disputation and textual analysis and embraced modernity. My mother was proud to be a Litvak and she looked down on the other branch of Eastern European Jewry, who are called Galitzianers, after Galicia, the region encompassing parts of Poland and the Ukraine where the Hasidic strain of Judaism emerged in the eighteenth century. (Recently, I learned that the paternal side of my family is, in fact, Galitzianer: my father's father was born into the Ger Hasidic sect in Bialystok, Poland, although he later turned his back on Hasidism.)

My mother's enmity to Hasidism stemmed from her incipient feminism. She did not like the way women were treated in the Hasidic world—having their heads shaved when they married, being required to remain at home, birthing baby after baby. (It particularly galled her that Hasidic men would not shake a woman's proffered hand.) All Galitzianers were not Hasids, but Jews from this region have traditionally practiced a conservative, folkloric, heartfelt form of Judaism. (The Litvak version of Judaism is criticized by some as overly intellectual.) Reading Mark Russ Federman's *Russ & Daughters*, which tells the story of his family's beloved Lower East Side "appetizing" store, I learned to my surprise that the Galitzianers, of which Federman is one, sneered right back at the Litvaks—this was a part of the story that my mother never told me. Prejudice, it would appear, exists inside and outside the Jewish tent.

In 2012, as I planned our trip to Eastern Europe, my knowledge of Jewish history and geography was decidedly spotty. In my mind Lithuania was the center of the Jewish/Litvak world and Vilniua, the center of the center. The truth was a bit more nuanced. Prior to World War II, Vilnius ("Vilna" in Yiddish) was a predominantly Jewish city and a hugely important center of the Yiddish language, as well as Jewish culture and art.

The fact that Jews in Lithuania fared very badly during World War II felt personal to me. In retrospect, I see that I arrived in Vilnius with a chip on my shoulder.

92. Coo-Coo in Vilnius

Our hotel in Vilnius abutted a sixteenth-century stone wall built to repulse outsiders, a mission our hotel continued to embrace. Tall and narrow, with a steep central staircase, a cramped lobby, and tan walls, the hotel oozed communist-era suspicion. The poker-faced receptionist who scrutinized our passports paused to scowl at mine, making me wonder if she knew from my name, or from my nose, that I was Jewish. She returned both passports to John and then gave him a large iron room key attached to an eight-inch wooden paddle. We were to leave the key at the front desk when we went out. "It is forbidden," she said in faltering English, "to remove the key from the premises. Forbidden. *Verboten*."

Our top-floor room was clean and overlooked the city, but the large window had no shade, a serious oversight in a town where the sun barely sets in July.

The next morning, we didn't have a lot of time to spare as we headed to the lobby looking for the breakfast room—we were to meet our guide, Lina, in the courtyard in less than an hour. The day clerk directed us to the subbasement. We descended two steep, dimly lit flights of irregularly spaced stone stairs. Small boulders implanted in concrete extruded from the walls, taking up space in the stairwell, adding menace to claustrophobia. I found myself thinking about the despairing messages scratched into the walls of the medieval dungeon in France that we visited years ago to satisfy Noah's prepubescent love of gore.

"In case you haven't noticed, this stairway is the only way out of here," I said to John as we stepped into a large stone and concrete chamber. On one side, a small breakfast area with eight tables had been set up. On the other, a replica of a Munich beer hall, with a long bar carved from a tree trunk, huge wooden beer barrels, and swords and shields hanging on the wall. We sat at a table along the far wall. A few feet from us, a German-speaking guy in a sport jacket methodically consumed his morning meal, tense shoulders rising up to meet his ears. Next to us, a pair of skinny Brits drank coffee and spoke quietly to one another.

John asked what I wanted to eat.

"This room is appalling," I said using my teaching voice, the one that carries.

John said nothing.

"Unspeakable things happened here. I can feel it," I said.

"What do you want to eat?" John repeated.

"I can't breathe," I said. I needed John or someone to acknowledge the pervasive sense of menace squeezing the breath from my lungs.

"This room reminds me of the basement cell where Josef Fritzl held his daughter captive for twenty-four years," I said.

"That was Austria," John interrupted.

"Her father raped and tortured her. Her name was Elisabeth. She gave birth to seven babies in that dungeon."

The maid set coffee and a breadbasket in front of me.

"For twenty-four years no one came to her rescue, not even her mother," I said.

I felt like a character in a Stephen King story. Horror had revealed itself to me and I had to speak. Had to convince John and all those present that danger, imminent danger lurked in the corners. "Do you know what happened to Lucy Dawidowicz's friends in this awful city?" I said, referencing the memoir by the Holocaust historian that I had recently been reading, then intoned in a Shakespearean voice, "Death. Death. Death."

"I think you had better leave," John hissed.

I took my coffee and toast upstairs to the garden, where I seated myself at a table underneath an arbor of fragrant linden trees.

The waitress from the breakfast room looked frightened as she approached me saying something that sounded like "oom-looot." I wondered if she was telling me that "it is forbidden" to sit in the garden. After she scurried away, I realized that she was asking if I would like an omelet.

The natural light pouring into my eyeballs returned me to my senses and I started to feel squirmy about my outburst.

At nine on the dot Lina, a former nuclear scientist who left that field to become a sought-after guide and archivist, found me in the garden. Lina earned a good living—and made a huge contribution—organizing tours in Lithuania for journalists, authors, researchers, and roots-seeking American Jews. She was recommended to me by a historian I knew based in South Carolina. Though a hot, sunny day was predicted, Lina wore a dark long-sleeved shirt with a sweater tied around her neck and a long black skirt that skimmed her Birkenstocks, only occasionally revealing her white socks. Attached to her over-sized orange rucksack was a safari hat. She looked like a hippie version of a nineteenth-century British lady prepared to ride sidesaddle across the dessert.

I asked if she would like some coffee.

She preferred tea.

If the hotel was a nightmare dimly remembered, Lina was a distant cousin recalled though a glass darkly. She spoke excellent English, with what sounded to me like a thick Yiddish accent. She did speak Yiddish. And Lithuanian and Russian and a bunch of other languages. Her father, she told me, was a Russian Jewish doctor from Stalingrad who settled in Vilnius after World War II and died there from the lingering effects of wartime starvation; her mother was Lithuanian.

Lina bent down, picked up her worn backpack, and began unzipping its compartments. Like clowns tumbling from a clown car, containers holding bits of last night's dinner appeared on the table in front of me. "Here," she said insistently, "You must taste my mother's potato latkes." Potato latkes? The quick transition from Stephen King to Woody Allen disoriented my already disordered brain.

Sitting in the garden waiting for John, Lina and I quickly covered a lot of territory. Her family. My family. Her work as a guide and archivist. My work as a writer. In the thrall of new best-friend-dom, I felt compelled to confess my morning misbehavior. I had fallen under the spell of Lucy Dawidowicz's memoir *From that Time and Place*, I explained, earlier in the month while visiting Zaragoza, Spain, with John—he was there to attend a European nanotechnology workshop, I was there as a spousal plus-one. In Zaragoza, I had spent the mornings exploring. In the afternoon I had retreated to our hotel room to escape the relentless Spanish sun. Floor to ceiling brocade drapes pulled shut, I dove deep into Dawidowicz's description of studying Yiddish literature and language in Vilnius; meeting poets, journalists, and scholars, attending the theater, drinking wine, and forging friendships she expected to last a lifetime.

Dawidowicz lingered in Vilnius throughout the summer of 1939, despite the growing threat of war. On August 23, 1939, Germany and Russia signed their infamous nonaggression pact. One week later, Germany invaded Poland. Europe was at war and escape routes were slamming shut. Her American passport enabled Dawidowicz to travel from Vilnius, through Poland, to Copenhagen, where on September 16 she boarded one of the last civilian ships sailing from Northern Europe to Boston. When the Nazis arrived in Vilnius the following year, they and their collaborators murdered more than 70,000 of the city's Jews, including Dawidowicz's friends. In her memoir, she described the hatred she felt for the Nazis and their supporters and her furious desire for vengeance. She wrote that she was happy when the Allies bombed German cities, incinerating 600,000 civilians. These were noncombatants. Women and children. Her naked hatred—an eyewitness's response to history—humbled me.

I told Lina how unsettling it was to be in Vilnius after reading this book. The resulting sense of inner dislocation, I suggested, led to my outburst in the breakfast room. The approval I was looking for did not register on Lina's face. She wasn't buying my story. She looked at me. "You mean you were *meshuga*," she said, using the Yiddish word for "crazy," and though her sentence rose at the end, it really wasn't a question.

I tried once again to explain. From Spain, I told her, John and I had traveled to Berlin. "A modern city built on a necropolis,"

I said. Lina again looked at me with skepticism. "You read too many books," she said.

93. The Weight of History

John arrived and we set out on our day's explorations. We spent an hour admiring the city's Roman Catholic cathedral built on top of a pagan temple—John, as always, preferred the pagan version of the story. After, we embarked on a day of nonstop dead Jews. At the Vilna Gaon Museum of Jewish History we pondered the photographs of prosperous and accomplished-looking families, all shot, bludgeoned, gassed, or starved to death. At the ruins of the city's magnificent Great Synagogue, we contemplated the destruction of 450 years of Jewish culture, religion, and history. A visit to the Vilnius ghetto? Everybody knows what happened there. And then we climbed into our rental and drove to the countryside, to see desecrated Jewish graveyards. The barn at Pirčiupiai where so many people—119 Jewish men, women, and children—were burned alive. All the stories were the same. Death, followed by the theft of Jewish property. It went on and on for nine unbearable hours.

What was one to do with such knowledge? I asked, on our ride back to Vilnius. "How should one react to 'this valley of dying stars . . . this broken jaw of our lost kingdoms'?"

Lina scowled at me. "Don't start with the poetry," she said.

94. A Jaundiced Assessment

The next day, Lina arrived early as I was eating a boiled egg in the hotel garden. Once again, she tried to fill my plate with unwanted leftovers.

When I refused, she told me that she had been thinking about my misbehavior the previous day. "This isn't a five-star hotel," she said. "It's a three-star hotel. It doesn't have a dining room with white tablecloths. If you wanted that, you should have stayed at the Grand Hotel Kempinski. I think you acted like a spoiled American brat," she told me.

There was nothing to say, so I said nothing, noting to myself that now I was traveling with not one but two disapproving moralists.

95. Lithuanian Rye Bread

Day two of our tour with Lina we focused on Lithuanian rye bread. In the afternoon we drove to the Open-Air Museum of Lithuania, where Lina had arranged for us to meet the director, who spent hours explaining how artifacts from different regions of Lithuania were used in the harvesting and threshing of rye and other grain and in the baking of bread. Lithuanian rye bread is less sweet and sour than Latvian rye and it is often made with scalded milk, rather than water. Ground carrots, potatoes, or cabbage are sometimes added to extend short supplies of grain. Adding root vegetables to bread dough occurs throughout the Baltics, but the practice is most associated with Lithuania. Lithuanian potato bread is particularly well known—not only do the potatoes enable the baker to use less rye, but dough that combines rye flour with mashed potatoes is easier to work than breads with higher percentages of rye flour.

Culturally, too, there are big differences. In Lithuania, bread baking is closely associated with Catholicism and the Roman Catholic veneration of Saint Agatha, the patron saint of the hearth and bakers. Lithuanians built shrines dedicated to Saint Agatha on roadways leading into villages and towns, imploring the saint to protect their homesteads from catching fire. Just down the road in Latvia, on the other hand, scholars, bakers, and ordinary people associate growing rye and baking rye bread with their country's ancient pagan belief system. Rye bread in Latvia has long been celebrated as local, indigenous, unrelated to the Livonian Order of the Teutonic Knights who Christianized Latvia 800 years ago, opening the door for the theft of Latvian land by German land barons. Whether or not they consider themselves Christians, whether or not they are members of the state-established Lutheran church, Latvians commonly associate rye bread with the nature-worshipping pre-Christian past.

96. Cleansed

We left the Open-Air Museum late in the day and drove to the town of Trakai, home to an odd sect of Turkic Jews called Karaites, only 200 of whom were still living there. The Karaites cooperated with the Germans during World War II and several hundred served in the German armed forces. Wrap your mind around that one. When we arrived at Trakai Island Castle, located in the middle of a lake, it was after 8 p.m., and the castle and its museum were closed for the day. We decided to take advantage of the lovely lake and swim. John cannot tolerate cold water—he has too little body fat. He swam a few dozen meters then stood talking with Lina in thigh-high water.

Swimming out into the lake, far from Lina's piercing assessment of my character, far from history and from John's judgments and prejudices, far from everything except my left arm and then my right, slicing cleanly and rhythmically through the clear cold water, I could finally breathe freely. Time ceased as I swam toward the setting sun. Alone and unweighted, my foolishness and the burden of all we had seen these past days washed away, and I was cleansed.

On the drive back to Vilnius, we passed a road sign written in English that read THIS WAY TO MINSK. I laughed out loud. Both of my mother's parents were born in the province of Minsk. If they hadn't fled, both sides of my mother's family most likely would have died in Minsk. In a certain sense I was closer to my roots than I had ever been. And yet that home was not my home, and it never would be.

97. Misappropriation

Immersed in the hot tub at Wilson High School in the District of Columbia after swimming laps a few years ago, I told my friend Sarah about my misbehavior in Lithuania. Sarah is English; we teach writing together. I take pride in my ability to tell a story, but in this case, I must have rushed the punch line, arriving prematurely at the moment when Lina called me a spoiled American brat, because Sarah didn't get it. Trying to explain, I told her that my misbehavior in the hotel breakfast room amounted to an act of "historical misappropriation." I appropriated—took ownership of—a story that was not fully mine. Yes, I told her earnestly, I am Jewish. And yes, I am a Litvak, a Russian Jew. And, of course, I have strong feelings about the murder of innocents, especially Jews, especially writers, especially children. But having been born after the war, on this side of the Atlantic, in a time and place of safety and prosperity, the Holocaust was not my story. Given my privileged position, I said, it was my responsibility to bear witness quietly, humbly recognizing the capriciousness of a fire that consumed some and spared others. When addressing such a morally serious topic: best to can the melodrama.

JOHN HAS POINTED out that I am often eloquent when I am wrong.

Do I still believe what I told Sarah that afternoon? That the Holocaust was not my story? Not exactly. Recently I have been rethinking my family's place in the stream of Jewish history. I now believe that my parents lied to themselves and to their daughters when they failed to acknowledge the tragedy that had befallen scores, maybe hundreds, of unknown relatives from both sides of our family . . .

My family was not exempt.

Ironically, Sarah, a woman who knew few Jewish people until she moved to the United States, intuited long before I that my sense of immunity was a defense. I wonder if she also understood that it was the unexamined nature of my emotions that caused me to behave so theatrically?

98. Our Guide Inessa

Lina hooked us up with a friend of hers in Latvia, a guide who specialized in taking Americans to visit the sites of

Jewish Riga. Strictly speaking, Inessa wasn't Latvian: she was a Russian Jew with a PhD in history who had grown up in Latvia. She lived half the year in Riga, and half the year in Moscow with her husband, a lawyer, who was not Jewish. Moments after meeting us, Inessa purposely let slip that her husband had recently bought her a Jaguar. That need to display one's wealth: we encountered it often among those newly introduced to capitalism.

Inessa began our tour at the ruin of Riga's Great Choral Synagogue, the site of what is commonly believed to be the first mass murder of Latvian Jews during World War II. Other historians dispute this fact, saying the victims were Jews from Lithuania, hundreds of them, who were hiding in the synagogue. Not in dispute is the nationality of the assailants: They were Latvian ultranationalists, not Germans, who locked the victims, whether Latvian or Lithuanian, in the synagogue, poured gasoline around the perimeter, and set the building ablaze, shooting to death all who tried to escape.

Near what had been the synagogue was a memorial commemorating those who died there. Adjacent to that memorial was a second commemorative plaque, this one honoring three hundred non-Jewish Latvians who protected Jews during the war, often at the cost of their own lives and sometimes at the cost of family members' lives. Most notable among them, the multitalented Jan Lipke, a resourceful fellow who earned his living as a dockworker and occasional smuggler. Lipke, along with his wife Johana, plus a band of helpers, saved at least forty Jewish people and perhaps more from certain death. In

Israel the names of the Lipke family and all the Latvian heroes who saved Jewish lives are inscribed in the list of the Righteous Among the Nations at the Yad Vashem Holocaust memorial in Jerusalem.

(I have recently read Dara Horn's brilliant book of essays, *People Love Dead Jews*, decrying the degree of attention paid to those memorialized at Righteous Among the Nations, the non-Jews who risked their lives to save Jews during the war. Focusing on the decency and courage of the very very few, she believes, prevents us from facing the historical truth dead-on: that Hitler almost completely succeeded in his effort to exterminate Eastern European Jewry. I both agree and disagree with her. Truly, we need to gaze at the burning sun, but we also need to turn away before we are blinded. Stories of hope, so long as they are not sentimentalized, are important.)

99. The Riga Ghetto

Inessa, John, and I ate lunch at a café in what had been the Jewish Ghetto, the neighborhood where Latvian Jews were warehoused by German Nazis before they were exterminated. The area is now quite swish and it thronged with tourists and locals enjoying the charms of the summer day. The weirdness of it all froze my heart. We chatted with Inessa about her fondness for Riga. She especially loved the city's restaurants and the food, which she described as fresher and more varied than what was generally available in Moscow.

The subject of food resonated. A few weeks before our trip, John had told me that Oma had told him that Jews kept Kosher because they thought they were too good to eat the same food everyone else ate—this, of course, is not true, but it was illuminating to me. John did not dispute his mother's opinion; in fact, he seemed to embrace it, which didn't surprise me given that more than once when I, say, refused to eat an overly ripe banana, John asked if I was "saving the banana for the Goyim." My husband and mate, the man I loved who undoubtedly loved me, seemed to believe my sense of myself as Jewish caused me to reject overly ripe fruit.

In that most recent occasion, I fought back, responding earnestly, explaining to John that Oma had misinterpreted the laws of Kashrut. Jews don't feel superior to other people, I said. When Jews came to America, they suffered from low self-esteem as a result of being different. They wanted to be like everyone else. They envied Christians. They wanted to eat bacon and celebrate Christmas. On and on I went, making the case that American Jews were a wounded lot. (And in truth, we are the people who birthed Freud and linguistically, if not literally, invented neurosis.)

John seemed to buy what I was saying, although when I am speechifying, I can never tell if he is really listening.

Then over lunch, Inessa seemed to confirm the stereotype: she told us that the year before she and her family had visited Israel, and she didn't like that country one bit. Her reason? "Here in Latvia," she said with conviction, "We Jews are better educated, more successful, and more cultured than other groups." In Latvia, she explained, she felt special. In Israel, she was just another ordinary person. Nothing special about her. And that kinship with ordinary folks? Definitely not to her liking.

100. Folly Not Withstanding

I want to be clear: Inessa's delight in her own imagined superiority does not diminish the monumental catastrophe that befell Jews in Latvia during World War II. The stories I tell of human vanity—hers and mine—do not alter the past's unbearable ugliness. Nor do they lift blame off the shoulders of the guilty. My stories merely illuminate how difficult it is when trying to understand the past to move beyond one's own very human preconceptions, prejudices, and projections. History cleanses the victims: the rest of us are condemned to live with our own blinding delusions.

As to feelings of superiority: Kindly name a group that on one level or another does not believe themselves superior to others?

Does John, as a Latvian, feel superior?

Of course, he does.

101. In the Krūmiņš's Garden (2012)

On a beautiful July afternoon in a garden on the Baltic Sea, we drank white wine and ate rye bread with smoked salmon with three generations of the Krūmiņš family. Iveta Krūmiņš and her husband, Bertrams, are political exiles the same age as John who formerly lived in Newtonville, less than a mile from our old house. John and Bertrams have known each since childhood—their fathers were friends. Their daughter and Ilze are friends. Iveta is smart and kind, and when our paths crossed, we would talk. That afternoon Iveta sat next to me. Growing tipsy on white wine, she leaned in to share a confidence. She told me something I have long known: that members of the Latvian émigré community in Boston were shocked and disapproving of John's and my marriage. They could not understand why Jānis would marry me, a non-Latvian and a Jew, less charming and beautiful (in their eyes) than his first wife. "But you know," she said expansively, "sometimes men just love their second wives more." I was gratified by this remark, but also bemused. Gratified to hear the success of our marriage acknowledged. Bemused that she attributed the success of our marriage to the fact that I am Wife Number Two. I was tempted to explain that it is the nature of John's and my relationship, not the fact that I am Wife Number Two, that binds us together. Instead, I patted her hand, smiled, and drank some more wine. I did this to honor the longevity of the family connection, the intimacy of her disclosure, and because I liked her. I also liked and admired her American-born children—her daughter, and her son, who, following the collapse of the former Soviet Union, quit his graduate program in history and moved to Latvia, where he met a Latvian woman with whom he started a newspaper devoted to news instead of propaganda—and I found her Latvian-born grandchildren lively and delightful, and on top of all of that, I was grateful—truly grateful—to be present and included.

102. Oma's Secret

One evening at dinner, after we returned, John told me a story about his mother that he had not previously shared.

He led into this tale by reminding me that Oma had employed three women in her pharmacy, and they were all Jewish. The first of the helpers was Miss Mahler. She was a Zionist. If a customer made an anti-Semitic remark in front of Miss Mahler, she would draw herself up straight and say proudly, "I am Jewish." Miss Mahler emigrated to Palestine before the start of the war. Miss Berlin was the second helper. John couldn't remember much about her. The third helper was Miss Rubenstein. After the Russian occupation in 1940, Oma noticed that Miss Rubenstein had become very curious about the people and the goings-on in the village. Moreover, she was writing many letters. Oma suspected she was sending information to the communist authorities in Riga. Later Miss Rubenstein became an employee of the communist bureaucracy in charge of pharmacies and was responsible for the national-ization of Oma's business. Throughout the nationalization pro-cess Oma was not treated unfairly; rather, she was left alone to run the pharmacy, though she no longer owned it.

John told me that Oma suspected that the information Miss Rubenstein provided the Russians may have led to the Siberian deportation of some of her neighbors in 1941. This statement is more freighted than one might imagine. Throughout the history of Jewry in Eastern Europe, Jews have so often been accused of being fifth columnists disloyal to local populations, pursu-ing their own nefarious, political, and money-making interests. If Miss Rubenstein were a devoted communist of the Leninist variety, which she may have been, perhaps she did denounce Oma's neighbors in Lielvārde; or perhaps those letters were written to relatives urging them to flee. We will never know. The assumption of Jewish guilt and Jewish disloyalty, however, is to be questioned unless proof is provided.

The Russians controlled Latvia for only a year. When the Germans marched into Latvia in 1941, Jews and those with communist and antifascist affiliations did their best to disappear. Oma could honestly say she did not know Miss Rubenstein's whereabouts when the local police chief stopped by to warn her that the Germans had ordered him to arrest Miss Rubenstein. A few days later Miss Rubenstein appeared at the pharmacy in a panic asking what should she do, where could she go? Oma had no answers, nor did she tell Miss Rubenstein that the local police chief had a warrant for her immediate arrest. She knew that if Miss Rubenstein were arrested, the Germans would torture her until she named those who had helped her. Instead, Oma told Miss Rubenstein that she would be safer in the countryside and she should leave Lielvārde at once.

Oma told John the story about Miss Rubenstein when he was in graduate school and seriously dating Maxine, who was Jewish. John wasn't sure what Oma was trying to convey to him, but when he and I decided to marry, Oma repeated this story, telling it to him as she had fifteen years earlier.

"Why do you think she told you this story?" I asked him. "What do you think it meant to her?"

"I think she wanted me to know that mixing ethnicities was more complicated than I knew," John answered.

"Do you think she was trying to warn you against marrying me?" I asked.

"No way," John answered. (And it's true that I never felt that Oma opposed our marriage.)

I asked John if he thought Oma felt guilty or complicit in relation to Miss Rubenstein? No. He did not. I found his answer improbable based on what I knew of human nature, but John would speculate no further. In point of fact, I identified with Oma, and I did not question her behavior. It seemed to me her primary responsibility was to safeguard her family, her children. She could hardly have been expected to hide Miss Rubenstein in her basement, the very space that soon housed a German communication center. Or am I giving her a free pass? Should she, like Jan Lipke, have forced herself to take a stand? This is the question I imagine she asked herself for the rest of her life. The question we all ask ourselves. What would we do if we were tested? Would our names appear among the Righteous of the Nations? Or would we do the sensible thing and protect ourselves and our families? Is it even moral to do what Lipke and Johana did, risking their children's lives for the lives of strangers?

103. Opa's Secret

The same evening John shared Oma's revelation about Miss Rubenstein, he told a story about his father, Jānis, who died before I came on the scene. During the Nazi occupation of Latvia, Jānis was the director of a flour mill, a job mired in ambiguity, as one of the Nazi's stated war policies was deliberate starvation of "inferior populations." As far as John knows, none of the mill workers were Jewish. Some, he believes, may have been Latvians who were paid a wage. Others were Russian prisoners of war. Once when his father was present, a large bag of flour split open after having been dropped accidently. He watched in horror as the Russians dropped to their knees and began shoveling fistfuls of raw flour into their mouths. (Telling this story years later, Jānis Senior broke down in tears.) Armed guards on duty at the mill rushed to the scene and beat them off with rifle butts.

His father, in John's telling, did the only thing he could do. He did nothing.

104. Complicity

What does it mean to go along with evil?

When does acquiescing become something worse?

Years after John told me these stories about his parents, I read the young French-German journalist Géraldine Schwarz's stunning family memoir *Those Who Forget*, documenting her grandfather's small-bore, bloodless, but consequential acts of compliance with the Nazi party and the Nazi regime in Mannheim, Germany. Reading this book helped me sort out what I think regarding the ongoing issue of wartime responsibility.

Schwarz's unflinching examination of her beloved grandfather's behavior, revealed in the boxes and boxes of written documents he hoarded until the day he died, told a deep, true story of a flawed, opportunistic man—decent in his own mind—seeking to save himself and his family. Though certainly not as bad as some, her grandfather's actions had significant and ultimately fatal consequences. He actively benefited financially and otherwise from the arrest and murder of Jewish friends and business partners. And he left proof of his misdeeds. Studying the past, revealing and remembering the past, required his granddaughter to tolerate knowledge about her own flesh and blood, a man she loved, that was intolerable. This for me is the heart of the matter: having the courage to look at oneself, one's loved ones, and the larger groups with which one is affiliated. To do so requires a person or people to understand that multiple histories exist side by side, and it requires, at times, that individuals be willing to remove the comforting cloak of their own victimhood, although they have indeed been victimized. Has such a reckoning taken place in Latvia? Some institutions and individuals have done this work, including Vaira Vīķe-Freiberga, president of Latvia from 1999 to 2007, a woman deeply interested in embracing all Latvian citizens, who after leaving the presidency joined Europe's Council of Toleration and Reconciliation. The larger record is less clear.

105. Giving Up His Tenure

In February 2014, on the eve of his seventy-fifth birthday, John retired from the University of Maryland, only he didn't call it that. John refused to say the "R word." "Giving up his tenure" is how he described his new circumstance.

Thanks to MIT and the University of Maryland and the rising stock market, we were okay financially. Not rich, but definitely not poor.

John's plan was to devote himself full time to Black Rooster Food in hopes of growing the company.

106. Convert

Like John, I now traveled with rye bread in my suitcase. Rye bread, ground coffee, and a one-cup Hario pourover with fluted filters for making coffee.

107. Weddings

Once upon a time I wanted to be a perfect stepmother and a perfect mother. Then two of our three married: Noah married Emily in 2013, and Ilze married Yücel in 2014. Now I wanted to be a perfect mother, a perfect stepmother, and a perfect mother-in-law.

I gave no thought to what it might feel like to have a writer, a writer with so much to say, as a mother, stepmother, and mother-in-law.

108. Sarma

After leaving banking, Sarma went to culinary school. Eventually she opened a successful restaurant in New York. She had other businesses, too. Noah, based in San Antonio, partnered with her on a venture that seemed quite promising. You can be wildly successful in the restaurant business and still be drowning in debt. Sarma was in over her head. A perfect target for a sociopath. She married the guy. He stole from her investors. She signed the paperwork. He had nothing to lose. She lost everything. The impact of her collapse ricocheted through our family, financially and otherwise.

109. 2016

Friends and acquaintances are left speechless when John tells them that 2016 was a dramatic year in the history of our family. "We got two grandchildren and a jail bird," he says as if reporting that one of our children had broken a leg while skiing.

Sarma pled guilty and served four months in prison, most of it in Rikers Island.

The husband, now an ex-, pled guilty and served a year in prison.

John was the only family member who visited Sarma at Rikers.

As to me, during the worst of the family drama, I found it difficult to think or write. I spent time in Brooklyn helping Ilze after the birth of her son. When Noah and Emily's daughter was born, I decided to rent an Airbnb for two months in San Antonio. Holding our tiny grandbabies—that's what comforted me.

110. Tested

I returned to Washington in early 2017. My brain functioned again, and I was able to finish a series of articles I had agreed to write updating my coffee book. It felt to me, however, as if our family's troubles were not ending. The outlays of money frightened me. I felt that John was choosing his youngest daughter over me. When I brought the subject up, he refused to engage. I found his silence unbearable. I decided that John and I had had a great run, but now it was over. Our marriage was kaput.

I spent a week out of the house. I worked all day in the DC Writer's Room, a coworking space where I was a member. I slept at home, but not in our bed. On a Friday evening in early spring, I was standing in front of my dresser getting ready for bed. John reached out to me. There were tears in his eyes. "You have no idea how hard this is for me. How torn I feel," he said. His words opened a space inside me. He wasn't choosing. He was, against his will, irrevocably torn. I could encompass that. I let myself be held by him. I gave way. The breach between us was over.

A few months later I told this story to Newt Pendleton, our financial advisor, a family-oriented guy whom I trust completely. "You know, Michaele," he said, "I would do as John did, going out on a limb for my little girl . . ."

His words helped me understand.

John was doing what fathers do for their daughters.

111. The Second Half of the Year

By the second half of 2017, our world began to right itself. I could think again. I undertook an entrepreneurial venture, turning our downstairs guest room, sitting room, and bath into an Airbnb rental with a separate entrance. You can credit our popularity and Superhost status to the free rye bread and specialty coffee.

112. Entering a Manic Phase

John was entering a manic phase.

Why was I always taken by surprise when this happened?

First the week of unsound sleep. After which, the preoccupation with war. And then the hostility toward me that moved from his making jokes about the inevitability of love and hate in marriage (a concept he learned from me) to his mouthing malign tropes associating me with the billionaire Steve Cohen, whose SAC Capital hedge fund was found guilty of insider trading in 2013 and fined $1.8 billion.

I try to tell him that this form of hate speech is hurtful.

"You are manic," I say to him in the kitchen, my words a balled-up accusation, the center of which contains my fear.

He tells me that my words are hurtful, too.

He's manic more often than he was in the past.

113. Glitter and Doom

Years before, we'd seen an exhibition at the Metropolitan Museum of Art called *Glitter and Doom,* focusing on German portrait painting between the two World Wars. John was blown away by this show. He insisted we buy the bound catalogue. Periodically he would bring up Otto Dix's unflattering 1921 portrait of his art dealer and loyal patron, the lawyer Dr. Fritz Glaser. Dix portrayed his friend as a stereotypical Jew, with small eyes, an oversized nose, a shapeless body, and ineffectual hands. In the Met catalogue, this depiction is interpreted politically: "In portraying his friend and patron as a defenseless Jew, Dix showed a remarkable awareness of the intensification of anti-Semitism in Germany at the early date of 1921." John agreed that the painting was political and foreshadowed what happened next in Germany. Nevertheless, he found reason to blame the victim. "He's never worked a day in his life," John said contemptuously, looking at Glaser's hands. Then he said the exhibition should be a wake-up call for American Jews, especially the rich ones who work on Wall Street.

114. Clogs Two

We've been married for thirty-five years, and when he is manic, he still brings up the fucking clogs, the ones I threw out when we lived on Page Road. Is that the worst he can say about me after all this time?

115. Fear

I thought when he retired, John would do a better job running Black Rooster Food, but that was not the case. The company brought out a side of John's personality I did not know. Having to make certain decisions—how, for example, to reorganize Black Rooster—undid him. He didn't trust his own instincts. He told me that he needed his partners (his friend Ken and his brother Ivars) to protect him from himself. In all our years of marriage, I had never heard him say something so self-doubting.

116. Chevy Chase Bathtub

I was lying on my orange yoga mat watching *The Mindy Project* while stretching my back and hips. It was nearly 10 p.m. In

February. During a cold snap. The temperature in the bedroom was barely tolerable.

John was working at his computer in his office across the hall. "How can you watch that stuff," he asked contemptuously as he entered the bedroom. This was not a question, and he didn't wait for an answer. "We need to open the bedroom windows now to cool down the bedroom. I can't sleep in a warm room," he said. He sounded like *Downton Abbey*'s Mr. Carson dressing down a housemaid.

"Don't open the window yet," I said. "Wait until I am ready for bed."

Long-simmering grievance seeped into John's tone: "It takes a long time for the room to cool down."

"Please don't open the window," I repeated, as he walked over to it. "You turned down the thermostat half an hour ago. It's cold in here already. I'm cold."

"You can't be cold. I'm not cold." John said, opening the window as far as it would go.

"I can't be cold because you're not cold? That's the punch line to a joke about Jewish mothers," I said, pausing briefly to prepare a fusillade of verbal shrapnel. "Haven't you noticed yet that you and I are not the same person? I get cold at night. My basal metabolism drops . . ." And then? And then? I looked up from the floor and I saw how beaten and weary John looked. Why have this stupid fight, I asked myself, when Thor of the North was simply acting like Thor of the North?

From this moment of silence, a compromise emerged. "When this show is over in fifteen minutes, I will take a hot bath, and you can open the window, turn on the attic fan, and cool down the room. My core temperature will rise in the bath and I will be able to withstand the cold in the bedroom as I get under the covers. In fact, I agree with you: a cold room is better for sleeping." This last statement, recognizing that John really does have a point, surprised even me.

John looked at me and said nothing. Then he lowered the window and exited stage left. A truce had been declared. He returned to his office, where he seated himself, shoulders hunched, in front of his computer, surrounded by a rat's nest of paper.

"Damn," John said. "Three invoices just disappeared off the spreadsheet. This has been happening for the last half hour."

"I don't know why you do this kind of work so late at night," I said. "Your brain will function better in the morning."

"These invoices need to go out first thing and besides, in the morning I need to drive to Germantown to pick up bread." (John's baker's trucker dropped off a week's supply for John's Washington customers at a Russian grocery store about thirty minutes north of our house. After the pickup, John distributed the bread to his customers.)

John was struggling. I knew that. And so, I ran the bath.

Soon every part of me except my head was immersed in steamy water and lavender scented bubbles. I thought about John and me. The predictability of our fights: The thermostat (a fight so old that I inherited it from his first wife). The fight over seatbelts—must he always hit the accelerator before mine is fastened? The fight over my pronating ankles—he refused to believe that to protect my knees and hips, I must order new running shoes every six or eight months. "You need to walk softly, like a forest-dweller in moccasins," he tells me without an ounce of irony.

His moralizing infuriates me. My alleged profligacy infuriates hm. And the later the hour, the more irritated we become with one another. Our fights are not linear, and they are never resolved. And they vary very little.

How does one extract oneself from this cycle?

I had recently asked my friend Bob Winer this very question. Bob, a psychoanalyst, founded and co-leads New Directions, the writing program with which I have long been associated and for which I lead writing workshops. Bob treats couples and he was himself long married. Sitting in Bob's office—as a friend, not a patient—I asked him if he thought couples ever resolved their issues. After a moment of silence, he answered, no, he didn't think so. Not in the sense of resolve/dissolve. "But if they are lucky," he said, "over time partners become more compassionate toward one another."

I lifted myself out of the tub. Standing on the bathmat, I leaned over and opened the bathroom door, and called out to John.

"The water is nice and hot," I said. "Why don't you join me in the tub?

"I was hoping you would ask," John answered.

117. Marriage: The Last Definition

Marriage: A long-term relationship between individuals who,

if they are lucky, become more compassionate toward one another as the years pass.

118. Read My Mind

I made orecchiette with rapini and sausage for dinner on Sunday evening, going light on the red pepper flakes because John doesn't like spicy food. Still, this is one of my favorite pasta dishes. John and I listened to music as we ate. Yo-Yo Ma playing Bach's cello suites. "I much prefer the cello to the violin," John said.

"Me too," I said, emphatically and we both laughed. (As a music critic, I am up there with the guy who sneers at a painting, saying I don't know much about art, but I know what I like.)

We drank a second glass of Rioja.

Then John disappeared into his office to finish something he described as urgent and I started cleaning up. Not a huge job, but still there were three pots and pans and the salad bowl. Annoyance crawled up my craw as I cleared the table. I walked down the hall to John's office. I stood at his door. "Why am I cleaning up alone?" I asked. (Usually, I cook and John cleans up, although if we have guests or there are a lot of dishes, I help because, really, who wants to face a dirty kitchen alone when you are tired?)

Scowling, John rose from his desk chair. He didn't say a word. Just marched down the hall to the kitchen. I escaped into the bedroom and closed the door. I spent the next hour doing the *New York Times* Spelling Bee puzzle and watching the Golden Globes. Only one win for *If Beale Street Could*

Talk, but I aced the puzzle, so I was happy. John returned to his office after cleaning up.

At 11 p.m. he came to the bedroom muttering unhappily. He had promised a Latvian friend that he would translate some song lyrics, scan them, and email them back to her. It all took longer than he expected. The scanner didn't work right. The software directions were incomprehensible. The technology, plotting his ruination. (So odd to me that a guy who was a leader in an alternative technology for making microchips can't operate a printer.)

"If you had told me you had a job to do, I would have been happy to clean up by myself," I said. We were standing very close.

"I didn't ask for your help. I just wanted you to know what I was feeling."

"Sometimes I can read your mind," I said. "But this time I had no idea."

He threw his arms around me and drew me toward him. His face was pleasantly warm.

"I'm just so angry at myself," he said, "for making this so difficult."

I was silent for a long time. We stood there holding one another.

"You were listening," I said. "I didn't know you were listening."

119. Chemical Intervention

The psychiatrist who had been providing John with meds was clueless. I reached out to my various networks and helped John find a new psychiatrist, a retired government researcher—a scientist like John—who specialized in bipolar illness and took Medicare. The new guy, Eliot, is a gem. Moreover, he likes John. A new medicine prescribed by Eliot, and I am once again living with a man who understands the peanut butter sandwich joke.

120. Yes, But

The new medicine helps, it really does. But it does not alter the fact that, as he has aged, John's mood swings have grown more common. When John's mood swings, I retreat. When I pull away, he is so alone. When I don't pull away, his inability to see any point of view except his own infuriates me.

121. Dinner

You lose contact and then you find your way back to each other. John is especially good at this. He tells me I am beautiful. He tells me I have great legs. When I am cold toward him, he is affectionate and warm. We eat dinner together every evening. We drink a glass of wine. Sometimes the conversation is engaging. Sometimes, not. Sometimes we do puzzles. Or listen to music.

Although I love TV and John claims to hate it, when I watch something on PBS, HBO, or Netflix, John usually joins me.

There is comfort in proximity.

122. Grown Children

He is the only person in the world with whom you can obsess about your grown children. And you do obsess about these children, who are not the idealized beings you once imagined them to be. They have made choices. They have stumbled. You have stood by them and stood by each other. Trying to make things better, you, too, have made mistakes. Finally, you understand that no one is exempt. One way or another, everyone gets whacked. If you are lucky and if you are physically healthy—as thus far you have been, and your children have been—things get better.

123. Grandchildren
And again, if you are lucky, there are grandchildren. How besotted you are by these babies with their perfect skin and perfect trust and their sense of discovery and their gleeful laughs. In them, the world begins again. In them the cycle is revealed. In them your mortality is explained.

124. Which Is Not to Say
Which is not to say that John and I don't have work to do.
    We are not finished.

125. Contain Yourself
It is 2018. I have just returned home from a month-long writer's residency in Southwest France. I had expected to finish this book in France. But the allure of living in a tiny French village and the complexity of living with other artists derailed me. Partially derailed me. Now I am home, confronting a new set of complexities. Familial. Social. Financial. And the compelling necessity to complete this book. I twirl and whirl from

one set of tasks to another, overwhelmed and unsure. Then I default to the same old song and dance. "I am a worthless failure," I tell John. "I have never lived up to my potential and I never will because I let myself be consumed by other people." Then I burst into tears.

"Never say horrible things about yourself," John says mildly. Then he opens his arms and gives me a hug.

126. Molly Bloom Redux

He is older now.

White-haired and slender.

The triangulated chest and broad shoulders are less well articulated.

His belief (and mine) in his physical invincibility is eroding like ancient mortar worn away by time.

Still, he runs up the steepest hills in Rock Creek Park and aces all the math puzzles in the paper. Proof to himself and me that he is still in the race.

I continue to admire him, though his aging drives me crazy. It's frightening knowing what lies ahead.

In our life together, the kitchen looms large as ever. He doesn't cook, but he assembles—breakfast, lunch (grilled cheese on rye, still a favorite), hors d'oeuvres. I want him to be as speedy and efficient as he was in the past, but he is not. Cleaning up in the kitchen he does fine except for the scattered breadcrumbs, and I can live with that. Loading the dishwasher reveals the durability of his spatial intelligence. Tasks requiring organization and sequencing, they're a problem. (Aging, a wily foe, reduces performance where one is vulnerable, not where one is strong.)

And so it is on a Sunday morning in December, when Ilze and JonYücel, our two-year-old grandson, are visiting. Wrapping up a phone consultation with a writing student, I enter the kitchen where John has been making breakfast for the last half hour. "*Teti!* Rye bread!" JonYücel calls to his grandfather from the sunroom where Ilze has strapped him into his high chair and is feeding him slices of banana and orange.

Breakfast is not yet ready.

"Can I help?" I ask, as I peek into the waxed bakery bag containing four croissants—two plain and two chocolate—and two *canelés* (the small carmelized rum and vanilla pastries that are my favorite). Though he theoretically disapproves of pastry, John raced to the bakery this morning—and not just any bakery, Bread Furst, the best bakery—to purchase these treats fresh from the oven.

"Do you want me to put these out?" I ask.

"No, they are for dessert."

"Can I make the coffee?" I ask.

"I will make the coffee. You can make the horseradish sauce."

"Screw the horseradish sauce. There's cream cheese," I say, though my words lack conviction. This is not a fight worth having.

As I chop a shallot and assemble the ingredients for the sauce, I watch John slowly, artfully compose a platter of smoked fish garnished with dill fronds and lemon slices. Using his sharpest knife, he cuts into the tough, oily skin of a smoked whitefish, then carefully lifts a meaty chunk from its back. "There could be bones," he says.

We carry the fish platter, the horseradish sauce, the cream cheese, sweet butter, a basket of rye bread, a plate of sliced tomatoes and cucumbers, and a bowl of cut-up oranges and grapefruit into the sunroom.

We're almost ready to go, but still there is no coffee.

John hurries to the kitchen as JonYücel sets to work on a small plate of smoked salmon and rye bread. Our grandson loves rye bread. So does our granddaughter. Which is a damned good thing. At his bread demos John shows potential customers a video of Noah's eighteen-month-old daughter, Ellie, sitting in her high chair crowing wordlessly while gnawing on a slice of rye bread. "Teti bread," the babies call *rupjmaize*—Teti being our family's version of the Latvian word for father. (Our grandparent names are Teti and Bella—I chose Bella, which has no significance except I like the sound of it.)

"Do you want me to make the coffee?" I shout from the table.

"I will do it. The water is boiled. I've got everything laid out."

Using a small goosenecked can, John slowly pours hot water (200 degrees Fahrenheit) over twenty-four grams of freshly ground coffee nestled in an unbleached paper filter that sits on top of a ceramic pour-over. He makes coffee one cup at a time.

"What's taking so long?" I ask. My question, not a question.

"This cup is for Ilze, I want it to be perfect," John says.

Light pours through all the windows as I gaze at the beautiful abundance of healthy food on our table (with the croissants in hiding for dessert). John has made a special cup for Ilze: half caf and half decaf, plus frothed milk, just the way she likes it. Minutes later he serves a cup, all caf, to me. For himself: green tea. Finally, we are all together at the sunlit table. So many years. So many meals. I look at John and emotion like sunlight pours through me. I am so moved by this man. His unfathomable generosity. And I know I would do it all again. Despite differences that can never be dissolved, that can only be tolerated. I chose him and I choose him. This sudden illumination fills my heart and once again I say, yes. Yes. Yes. I will marry you and be with you and care for you and be cared for by you. Yes. I will.

EPILOGUE

IN 2021, JOHN found a young, energetic guy to be his partner in Black Rooster Food. Avery Robinson is thirty-two years old, a rye lover and rye baker. He is also an observant Jew with a big heart and a sense of humor. He has an interest in small business and a master's degree in Jewish Culinary History. He wrote his master's thesis on kugel. More important, since so far no one's getting rich selling rye bread, he has a day job.

I completed this book and have started another one. And I still teach writing.

Ilze and her husband Yücel, an artist and entrepreneur, are now settled in Vermont and have a son and a daughter. Ilze promotes global health and sustainability with the UN. Noah and his wife Emily—she teaches children with special needs and supervises other teachers—have a daughter and a son. Noah is a data scientist. Sarma works as a consultant and is writing a book. Turns out she is a very good writer. Sarma's longtime canine companion, Leon, eats clean and continues to thrive.

Our grandchildren sit down to dinner every night with their parents.

We are proud of that.

Of course, there are problems, but at this moment, all the members of our pod are doing okay, maybe, we hope, better than okay

But John and I, having been married for nearly forty years, we know nothing stays the same.

ACKNOWLEDGMENTS

AUTHORS NEED AGENTS and writers need editors and publishers. In all cases, I have enjoyed unusual good fortune. My agent Eleanor Jackson played, in her words, "a long game," with this book. "Memoirs take time," she told me. She was not wrong. Eleanor's patience, her belief in me, her judgment and her friendship, mean the world.

As to Abby Muller, the young Algonquin editor who acquired *The Rye Bread Marriage*: from Day One, Abby intuited where and how this book could be better, and acted as its champion. When she took another position, Abby arranged for my work to land on the desk of Algonquin's brilliant executive editor Amy Gash, who after careful reading urged me to rethink a few key passages. Superb advice I had the good sense to take.

Ellen Shapiro, fact checker, researcher, and arbiter of literary rectitude was unrelenting in her attention to detail and her quest for intellectual honesty.

Thanks to the talented team at Algonquin, including copy editor Chris Stamey, managing editor Brunson Hoole, and executive director of publicity Michael McKenzie. Working with you all has been a pleasure.

Publicist Extraordinaire Erin Cox is a get-it-done brainiac who laughs at my jokes.

Nested within *The Rye Bread Marriage* are numerous stories shared by lovers of rye bread in Latvia, Lithuania, Germany, and in the United States. In particular, I am grateful to the baker and oven builder Aivars Grinbergs, based in Lielevarde, Latvia, and to John's fellow Latvian emigree Maija Krustāns Šlesers, an artist and poet who lives in Newton, Mass. Their stories resonate profoundly. My thanks, as well, to Leon Swell, who opened doors to rye bread's New York past.

Many bakers and experts in Latvia met with John and me, taking time to talk with us and teach us while showering us with Latvian hospitality. These include the inestimable scholar Indra Čekstere, author of *Musu Maize: Our Daily Bread*, who has done so much to excavate and celebrate Latvia's glorious rye-bread-baking tradition. Special thanks, as well, to the Latvian Bakers Association, Riga; Lasma Bome, Lielezars Bakery, Limbaži; Juris Paulovičs, Ķelmēni Bakery, Ranka; Maris Šternbergs, Kuldiga Bakery, Kuldiga; and Normunds Skauģis, Lači Bakery, Babite.

I am grateful to our outstanding, multilingual Lithuanian guide, Regina Kopilevič, for educating me and setting me straight. And in Ulm, Germany, I am indebted to Dr. Andrea Fadana, director of the Museum of Bread Culture, who taught me vital lessons regarding bread's complex relation to human-kind. Other scholars, including Guntra Aistara, Hasia Diner, Stanley Ginsberg, Jeffrey Hamelman, Maruta Lietiņa Ray, Peter Reinhart, William Rubel, and Jane Ziegelman, gener-ously shared their knowledge. The kind reception and patient instruction I received at the European Reading Room of the

Library of Congress (housing 33,000 printed volumes from or about Latvia) opened worlds of knowledge to me.

I am indebted to two early scholarly readers: Indra Ekmanis, PhD, an expert in Baltic history, and Jewish culinary historian Avery Robinson, MA, the newest member of Black Rooster Food family.

Friends from every era of my life have found their way into this book. Some are named, others are present in the sinew. Always there is Carol Hymowitz, coauthor and bestie since freshman year. And Susan Blanchard, so generous. In Newton, Diana Altman and Richard Siegel; Jane Matlaw and all the Page Roadies; Susan and Larry Brill; and the neighborhood kids. These pals were rye bread's first non-Latvian fans.

In Washington glass artists Rhoda Baer, whose evolution has been an inspiration, and Heidi Lippman, who, like me, still quests; family members by choice, Motoko Shimizu and Henri Lezec; walking pals Willia Hennigan and Kathy Kretman; Brendan Doyle and Larry Kirkland, who had the effrontery to move away; fellow traveler and coteacher Sarah Pleydell, who is also in my essay-writing group; the inestimable Sally Swift. You guys, to use the noun favored by Sally, you guys assuage my cosmic loneliness.

Special callouts to our friend Mark Furstenberg, baker extraordinaire; to our neighbors Rob and Kelley Gronda, who stepped up when I needed recipes; to Nathalie Patel, who provided me with a temporary office; and to Peter Giuliano, the ultimate coffee guy and food scholar.

And then there are the members of my small but mighty essay-writing group: Nancy Arbuthnot, Sarah Pleydell, Lauren

Francis-Sharma, and Alexandra Anastasia Viets. Talented fellow writers, steady in their purpose, who help me to move forward.

Kudos to the Virginia Center for the Creative Arts (VCCA), where twice (first in Amherst, Virginia, and later in Auvillar, France) I holed up to write. In Amherst I met Paul Skenazy, who told me I would be okay if I stuck with the bread.

Thanks to Jeff Bailey, who liked my work, and to Liz Poliner, who thought the book was good.

Thanks to Robert Winer, MD, founding director of New Directions, for his wisdom regarding long-term marriage.

Thanks to the Rutins and the Viksnins, members of the Washington Latvian community, who welcomed me into the fold, and to Anita Juberts, Liana Eglītis, and Helēna Vīksniņa, who read the manuscript. Thanks, too, to the Boston- and Riga-based members of the Raudseps family and other members of John's folklore group in Boston, Piektvakara Puduris.

Thanks to the Melngailis clan here in the US, most especially Ivars and Ruta, and in Latvia, Nils Melngailis and Margita Melngaile, for their hospitality.

Thanks to our children and their spouses for tolerating a writer in the family. You and the grandbabes are my anchor.

A special shout-out to Mark Ellen Hood and Mark Petty, because writers have bodies that need tending.

The last word belongs, as always, to my husband, John Melngailis. As I had hoped, with you I became a world traveler. I am glad I said yes.

NOTES

PART ONE

3. Marriage: First Definition

p. 6 nourished by memories of a shared romantic past: I first
encountered this idea in Judith S. Wallerstein & Sandra Blakeslee,
The Good Marriage: How and Why Love Lasts (New York:
Houghton Mifflin, 1995) p. 322–26.

5. New York Bathtub (West Eighty-fourth Street, 1981)

p. 11 the cluelessness of young people like me: Russell Baker,
"Communicate, Dear Romeo," Sunday Observer, *New York Times*
(April 22, 1973).

13. Why John Called Himself a Pagan

p. 21 portions of modern-day Latvia and Estonia were forcibly
Christianized: Henricus Lettus, *The Chronicle of Henry of
Livonia*, trans. James A. Brundage, (New York: Columbia
University Press, 2003), p. 5.

16. Dainas 1

p. 24 vehicles of memory: Yosef Hayim Yerushalmi, *Zakhor: Jewish
History and Jewish Memory* (Seattle: University of Washington
Press, 1996 edition), p. xxix.
p. 24 folklore served to create a national identity: Edmunds V.
Bunkše, "Latvian Folkloristics," *Journal of American Folklore*
92, no. 36 (published by the American Folklore Society, April-June
1979), p. 204.

p. 25 the vessels of their soul: Saulcerite Vierce, *Kristjanis Barons: The Man and His Work* (Moscow: Raduga Publishers, 1985; English trans.), p. 126.

17. Dainas 2

p. 25 written in the morning of the world: Algirdas Landsbergis and Clark Mills, eds., *The Green Linden: Selected Lithuanian Folk Songs*. foreword by Robert Payne (New York: Voyages Press, 1964), p. 7.

18. Dainas 3

p. 25 Dievs was striding through the rye field: Saulcerite Vierce, p. 160.

p. 26 God grant that I should die: Saulcerite Vierce, p. 161.

p. 26 he wanted no monument to be erected: Saulcerite Vierce, p. 163.

19. Carriage House

p. 27 Latvians are as bound to place: E. V. Bunkše, "God, Thine Earth Is Burning: Nature Attitudes and the Latvian Drive for Independence," *GeoJournal* 26-2 (February 1992), p. 203.

43. Gourmet Food for Babies

p. 55 Julee Rosso and Sheila Lukins. *The Silver Palate Cookbook* (New York: Workman Publishing, 1979).

57. Chewing

p. 72 chewing "slows me down": Maria Speck, "A Gift of Grains," *Gastronomica* 7, no. 4 (Fall 2007), p. 86.

PART TWO

1. The Imprint of the Past

p. 81 the imprint of the past: Roger Cohen, *The Girl from Human Street: Ghosts of Memory in a Jewish Family* (New York: Alfred A. Knopf, 2015) p. 23.

p. 81 new opportunity is only one side: Roger Cohen, p. 27.

7. The Hegira (Riga, 1944)

p. 86 Timothy Snyder, *Bloodlands: Europe Between Hitler and Stalin* (New York: Basic Books, 2010)

10. Courtship

p. 89 Maynard Owen Williams, "Latvia, Home of the Letts," *National Geographic*, (October 1924), p. 401–43.

14. In the Line of Fire

p. 95 Ian Frazier opined in the *New Yorker*: Ian Frazier, "*On the Prison Highway*," *New Yorker* (August 23, 2010) p. 33–34.

18. Leaving the Sudentenland

p. 105 90 percent of Germany's rail capacity had been destroyed: Tony Judt, *Postwar: A History of Europe Since 1945* (New York: Penguin, 2005), p. 85.

20. Flashbulb Memories

p. 109 flashbulb memories: Art Markman, "The Consistency of Flashbulb Memories," *Psychology Today* (posted June 26, 2015). https://www.psychologytoday.com/us/blog/ulterior-motives/201506/the-consistency-flashbulb-memories

23. British Zone Food

p. 114 American farmers after World War II: Lizzie Collingham, *The Taste of War: World War Two and the Battle for Food* (London: Penguin, 2011) p. 476–84.

p. 114 "All thinking and feeling, all wishes and hopes began with food": Anonymous (Marta Hillers), *A Woman in Berlin*: Eight Weeks in the Conquered City; a Diary, trans. Phillip Boehm (London: Picador, 2006), p. 3.

40. Oma Learns to Bake Rye Bread (Butler, Pennsylvania, 1950)

p. 134 Ian Frazier, *Travels in Siberia* (New York: Farrar, Straus and Giroux, 2010), p. 406

42. Alfred Kazin 1

p. 136 "I worked on a hairline between triumph and catastrophe": Alfred Kazin, *A Walker in the City* (San Diego: Harcourt Books, Harvest paperback, 1979), p. 21.

PART THREE

2. Kahlil Gibran

p. 146 "work is love made visible": Kahlil Gibran, *The Prophet* (New York: Alfred A. Knopf, 1923).

3. Cultural Memory 1

p. 146 Aleida Assmann, *Cultural Memory and Western Civilization* (Cambridge University Press, 2011). https://www.youtube.com/watch?v=Hjw07_A--sg https://www.jstor.org/stable/488538

5. Stories about Home

p. 147 "Small is my dear home": E. V. Bunkše, "God, Thine Earth is Burning: Nature Attitudes and the Latvian Drive for Independence," *GeoJournal* 26-2 (February 1992), p. 208

p. 148 centuries-old Latvian yearning for a homeland: E. V. Bunkše, p. 209.

6. Stories about Work

p. 149 the experience of chronic hunger and extraordinary deprivation: Maruta Lietiņa Ray, "Recovering the Voice of the Oppressed: Master, Slave, and Serf in the Baltic Provinces," *Journal of Baltic Studies* 34, no. 1 (Spring 2003), p. 11.

p. 149 "Whither shall I flee, Oh God": Uriah Katzenelenbogen, *The Daina: An Anthology of Lithuanian and Latvian Folk-songs* (Chicago: Lithuanian News Publishing Co., 1935), p. 143

p. 150 "Cursed by God": Uriah Katzenelenbogen, p. 97.

8. Stories about Threshing Rye in Heaven and in Hell

p. 151 "Cough and cough continually": Uriah Katzenelenbogen, p. 143.

p. 151 "My cheeks are so pale": Maruta Ray, p. 10.

9. Stories about Stoicism and Resilience

p. 151 "Sorrow, sorrow—oh sorrow": E. V. Bunkše, "God, Thine Earth is Burning: Nature Attitudes and the Latvian Drive for Independence," *GeoJournal* 26-2 (February 1992), p. 206

13. Reading the Text

p. 154 "Work is love made visible" Kahlil Gibran, *The Prophet.*

25. Rebecca at the Well (November 1996)

p. 161 "I'm still here": Stephen Sondheim, "I'm Still Here," (Nashville: Herald Square Music, 1971)

54. Zabar's

p. 183 pumpernickel is a coarse, almost crust-less rye bread: Stanley Ginsberg, *The Rye Baker: Classic Breads from Europe and America* (New York: W. W. Norton, 2016), p. 336–39.

59. Rye Bread Tutorial

p. 191 famed bread baker and cookbook writer Jeffrey Hamelman: https://food52.com/blog/25484-what-is-king-arthur-baking-company Jeffrey Hamelman, *Bread: A Baker's Book of Techniques and Recipes* (Hoboken, NJ: John Wiley & Sons, 2004).

60. Deprived

p. 192 resisting the Red Army's effort to turn their farms into large collectives: https://eng.lsm.lv/article/culture/history/kolkhozs-how-collectivization-changed-the-latvian-countryside-utterly.a299116/

68. Indra Čekstere and the Blue-Eyed Baker

p. 204 Indra Čekstere, *Mūsu Maize: Our Daily Bread; The Traditions of Latvian Baking* (Riga: Hanzas Maiznīcas, in collaboration with Latvian Ethnographic Open Air Museum, 2004)

69. Peter Reinhart

p. 206 Peter Reinhart's TED Talk: https://www.ted.com/talks/peter_reinhart_the_art_and_craft_of_bread?language=en Peter Reinhart, *Whole Grain Breads: New Techniques, Extraordinary Flavor* (New York: Ten Speed Press, 2007)

70. Holy and Eternal

p. 207 R. W. Apple, Jr., "The Miracle of Rye: In Germany, and Among Some Here, Rye Bread Is a Spiritual Thing," *New York Times* (July 15, 1998).

72. The Museum of Bread Culture (2012)

p. 208 The Museum of Bread Culture: http://www.eiselen-stiftung.de/museum-brotkultur-ulm-en.php

73. H. E. Jacob

p. 210 H. E. Jacob, *Six Thousand Years of Bread: Its Holy and Unholy History* (New York: Skyhorse Publishing, 2014; 70th ann. ed.)

74. William Rubel (2015)

p. 210 William Rubel, *Bread: A Global History* (London: Reaktion Books, 2011)

75. Research 1

p. 211 Having established that "starch grains, possibly in the form of flour": Anna Revedin et al, "Thirty Thousand-Year-Old Evidence of Plant Food Processing," *Proceedings of the National Academy of Sciences of the United States of America* 107, no. 44 (November 2, 2010), pp. 18,815–19.

76. Research 2

p. 212 "Thousands of years after our human": Stanley Ginsberg, *The Rye Baker*, pp. 14–18.

p. 213 William Rubel, *Bread: A Global History*, (London, Reaktion Books, 2011), pp. 43–44.

77. Taking Rye to Its Limit

p. 213 "There is something primal about rye breads": Stanley Ginsberg, *The Rye Baker*, p. 249.

p. 213 "Of all the [rye] breads of Eastern Europe, the breads of Latvia are held in highest regard.": Stanley Ginsberg, *The Rye Baker*, p. 261.

78. Bread of Our Fathers

p. 214 A deeper layer of rye baking: Stanley Ginsburg, *The Rye Baker*, p. 13.

p. 215 "the rye bread could stay fresh for weeks": Stanley Ginsberg and Norman Berg, *Inside the Jewish Bakery: Recipes and Memories from the Golden Age of Jewish Baking*, (Philadelphia: Camino Books, 2011), p. 56.

79. Jewish Hunger

p. 215 "a hunk of rye bread and a bit of herring": Abraham Cahan, *The Rise of David Levinsky*, (New York: Penguin Twentieth Century Classics, 1993), p. 6.

p. 215 Children had to nag their mothers for a piece of bread: Cahan, page 7.

80. Alfred Kazin 2

p. 215 Never had a chance to know what hunger meant: Alfred Kazin, *A Walker in the City* (San Diego: Harcourt Books, Harvest paperback, 1979), p. 32–33.

82. Leon Swell

p. 216 As to the presence of raisins: R. W. Apple, Jr., "The Miracle of Rye: In Germany, and Among Some Here, Rye Bread Is a Spiritual Thing," *New York Times* (July 15, 1998).

84. Jewish Food-Joy

p. 220 Jewish food-joy: Jane Ziegelman, *97 Orchard Street: An Edible History, of Five Immigrant Families in One New York Tenement*, (New York: Harper Collins, Smithsonian Books imprint, 2010), p. 119.

p. 221 in the elaborate system of culinary laws and rituals: Jane Ziegelman, p. 119.

p. 221 Always simmering in a Jewish eater's thoughts: Jane Ziegelman, p. 119.

85. Overdoing It

p. 221 the thrill bedazzled newcomers experienced: Hasia Diner, *Hungering for America: American, Irish, and Jewish Foodways in the Age of Migration* (Cambridge, Mass.: Harvard University Press, 2001), p. xvi

87. A Rationing Mentality

p. 224 the Latvian distaste for drama and hyperbole: E. V. Bunkše, "God, Thine Earth is Burning: Nature Attitudes and the Latvian Drive for Independence," *GeoJournal* 26-2 (February 1992), p. 207.

p. 224 a rationing mentality: Richard Tellström, introductory essay, in Magnus Nilsson, *The Nordic Cookbook* (London and New York: Phaidon Press, 2015), p. 27.

p. 225 "bread with an old soul": Richard Tellström, p. 27

92. Coo-Coo in Vilnius

p. 232 Lucy Dawidowicz, *From that Place and Time: A Memoir 1938–1947* (New York: W. W. Norton, 1989).

98. Our Guide Inessa

p. 240 Dara Horn, *People Love Dead Jews: Reports from a Haunted Present* (New York: W. W. Norton, 2021).

104. Complicity

p. 247 Géraldine Schwarz, *Those Who Forget: My Family's Story in Nazi Europe; a Memoir, a History, a Warning*, trans. Laura Marris (New York: Scribner, 2017).

113. Glitter and Doom

p. 252 in portraying his friend and patron as a defenseless Jew: Sabine Rewald, with essays by Ian Buruma and Matthias Eberle, *Glitter and Doom: German Portraits from the 1920s* (New York: Metropolitan Museum of Art, 2006), p.105.